Alligators, Prehistoric Presence in the American Landscape

CREATING THE NORTH AMERICAN LANDSCAPE

Gregory Conniff, Bonnie Loyd, Edward K. Muller, David Schuyler, *Consulting Editors*

Published in cooperation with the Center for American Places, Harrisonburg, Virginia

Martha A. Strawn

ALLIGATORS

Prehistoric Presence
in the American Landscape

with essays by
LeRoy Overstreet
Jane Gibson
J. Whitfield Gibbons

THE JOHNS HOPKINS UNIVERSITY PRESS
BALTIMORE AND LONDON

For Clifford E. Strawn

© 1997 Martha A. Strawn
Essays by LeRoy Overstreet, Jane Gibson, and J. Whitfield Gibbons
© 1997 The Johns Hopkins University Press
All rights reserved. Published 1997
Printed in Hong Kong on acid-free paper
06 05 04 03 02 01 00 99 98 97   5 4 3 2 1

The Johns Hopkins University Press
2715 North Charles Street
Baltimore, Maryland 21218-4319
The Johns Hopkins Press Ltd., London

Library of Congress Cataloging-in-Publication Data will be found
at the end of the book.
A catalog record for this book is available from the British Library.

ISBN 0-8018-5289-7

Contents

Preface

Raised in the Florida waterlands, I often went out with my father in search of edible plants and animals. We gathered avocado pears, small Florida bananas, swamp cabbage, coconuts, lychee nuts, pecans, oranges, grapefruit, sugarcane, papayas, mangoes, and melons of all kinds, especially the ever favorite watermelon. Occasionally we went to north Florida and Alabama to pick small purple figs and wild southern grapes called muscadines and scuppernongs. After these trips Mom and Dad spent days making preserves from whole figs and thin lemon slices, and from the grape hulls and their simmered-out pulp. Sometimes we also went hunting and fishing. I grew up eating fresh seafood and fish from the Gulf of Mexico and the Atlantic Ocean; frog legs and eels from southern lakes and rivers; wild rabbits, squirrels, ducks, quail, boars, and bears from the Florida sand hills and piney woods; and pheasants that my father and mother shot on yearly trips to the area around Bonesteel, South Dakota.

My father's early history colored our family life. He was raised in rural Alabama in the early 1900s and ate "store-bought" meat only after he grew up. Hunting, fishing, and gathering edible plants were a way of life for him. Though trained as a lawyer, he worked in real estate because he loved the land and nature, and that profession allowed him to work in places he enjoyed. He also was in a position to maintain or destroy environments. Issues of economic need and environmental quality thus were firsthand experiences in my life from an early age.

My father taught me to forage and hunt only for flora and fauna that would be eaten. His ethic was to maintain the natural balance of regeneration and to respect the dignity of the animals. He taught me to be aware of, to care for, and to honor all creatures and their habitats.

This book contains photographs of the southern aquatic landscape and the wildlife and human communities that depend on the land's riches for their livelihood and culture. In 1985 I directed a group of students photographing Florida's controlled alligator hunts and the people involved with them, including agency personnel of the Florida Game and Fresh Water Fish Commission (FGFC), research biologists, alligator hunters and their families, and alligator processors. Afterward I was able to work with the FGFC in creating a visual education package. The interdisciplinary nature of that work led me to conceive this project.

This book is first and foremost a photographic body of work structured in sequences, each based on a concept or feeling. The various sequences are designed to create a complete network of experiences. The pictures are complemented by essays, poems, song lyrics, and vignettes that flow around and along with the movement of the image sequencing. Like water in a stonebed creek, photographs and written materials form the book's framework.

The three written essays include the storytelling memoirs of an alligator hunter; a conservation anthropological account of a model fisheries community with the pseudonym Shellcracker Haven; and an ecological commentary based on the mythological and biological parity between alligators and people. The writers are LeRoy Overstreet, owner and operator of Little River Construction Company, Epes, Alabama, and nuisance alligator hunter with over fifty years' gator hunting experience in Florida and Alabama; Jane Gibson, Ph.D. conservation anthropologist, University of Kansas, Lawrence; and J. Whitfield Gibbons, Ph.D. ecologist and senior researcher, Savannah River Ecological Laboratory, Aiken, South Carolina, author of several books on ecology and syndicated columnist for the *Tuscaloosa News* and *New York Times*. All three are lucid, extremely well informed, original thinkers. Each has a distinctive personality and point of view.

In conceiving this work, I set out to present visual and written materials that are loosely associated but with neither illustrating the other. Thirty-two visual sequences vary in dynamic. Some are more impressionistic; others tend to follow an order of activity. None is developed to convey specific information as text might. The audience's experiences in interacting with the visual material that composes each sequence, and whose energy may appear as symbolic, contrasting, conflicting, or patterned, are primary in this work. The vignettes and essays are similarly designed, but they communicate through language. Although the book presents a large amount of carefully researched information, its greater goal is to create an experience that elicits feeling and understanding.

This book is meant to be more than the sum of its parts. As creator and concept designer, I chose to include various points of view, trusting that spectators/readers will take their own positions. My intention is not to under- or oversimplify matters, but to present a complicated scenario with one harmonious goal: to evoke a sense of place and convey the need for an American land ethic that recognizes the interdependence of humans and other animals in their joint and adjoining habitats. Although there is a unified conceptual goal, there are also varying approaches to that goal that are presented nonhierarchically. The book tells about people such as those who have developed school curricula, businesses, and festivals around alligators in Florida, Louisiana, and Texas because the livelihood of their communities depends heavily on alligators. It tells about historical and contemporary American Indian enterprises using alligators and other wildlife. And it tells about business and community support for wildlife conservation through individual commercial efforts such as Gatorland and the St. Augustine Alligator Farm, both in Florida, and the creation of groups to inform and educate, such as the American Alligator Cycle of Protection, founded by people in Florida's private enterprises who work as stewards of the wetlands and deepwater habitats.

This book is about information and dynamic beauty, about the special places in the American South where alligators live and thrive, and about the individuals, communities, and agencies that have helped to retain and maintain the balanced cycle of the alligators' existence. We live in a system that combines indigenous and artificial nature. The land ethic that people develop either by neglect or by intent will determine our future environment. I believe there is room for all creatures to thrive in their own habitats, sometimes sharing space, sometimes not; but always granting each other dignity and the right to live in a cycle of interaction that fosters our mutual well-being.

About the frontispiece: The verdant beauty of many of the Florida lakes is attributed to the contamination of the waters by fertilizers, which increase plant growth in the wetlands, choking the waterways. Another imbalance in the ecosystem which affects alligators that inhabit those waters is caused by DDE. A by-product of DDT breaking down in the environment, DDE mimics estrogen in its impact on animals and may be the cause of reduced productivity and increased size. The maximum length of a mature female is, historically, about nine feet. Recent fieldwork by southern biologists found three females in Lake Apopka in Florida that exceed nine feet, ten inches, thereby breaking previous records for live capture. Lake Apopka is heavily polluted with DDE and fertilizers. (Dicofol, a chemical compound with the brand name Kelthane, is the substance that spilled in Lake Apopka in Florida. Up to 15 percent of DDT can be Dicofol. This miticide is also applied to orange groves in areas near Lake Apopka. See Donald R. Clark, Jr., "Dicofol [Kelthane] as an Environmental Contaminant: A Review," Fish and Wildlife Technical Report no. 29, Washington, D.C., 1990.)

Alligators, Prehistoric Presence in the American Landscape

⫶⫶ Alligators in the American Landscape

Alligators are adapted primarily to aquatic habitats of the American South. They move gracefully and stealthily through the water but are relatively awkward on land, though they can charge quickly and aggressively. Alligators roam from one area to another during courtship or when the areas they inhabit become overcrowded by humans or other dominant alligators.

Crossing the white sands of the Florida landscape, through citrus and avocado groves, over highways in the Louisiana Cajun country and lawns and golf courses throughout the suburbanized South, alligators seek suitable habitats where they can feed, bask in the sun, perform courtship dances, mate, nest, and watch over their young. They are an enduring participant in the American landscape.

Remote in the Great Alligator Dismal Swamp area of North Carolina, which includes the Alligator River and the Alligator River National Wildlife Refuge (established in 1984) around Albemarle Sound, is a small lake inhabited by the American alligator (*Alligator mississippiensis*) and a pod of young, rare in this northernmost part of their range.[1] The Alligator River is connected to another remote lake, Alligator Lake (currently called New Lake) by the "Dunbar Ditch," formed, according to legend, when a meteor fell and created the lakebed,

pushing the ground up along the edges as it landed. The lakebed is "perched"; that is, the lake level is higher than the surrounding farmland.[2] Neil Glass, an area farmer, continues the story:

In 1985 when the big fire came through, the firefighters dug a ditch from the lake back into the field area and used the water to put out the fire. In early years, about 1756, there was a community of about twenty-five families around Alligator Lake, including the Dunbar family. Mary Dunbar was the last surviving person. She died in the early 1980s and is buried in a small graveyard nearby. A ditch called the

Dunbar Ditch was used to drain the land and to carry people by boat out to the Alligator River. There was no other access; the land around was too swampy for a road most of the year. More recently, since 1985, Jack Rose 'bout lost his dog to an alligator in the canal that runs from the Alligator River to the Intracoastal Waterway.

The original Great Alligator Dismal Swamp area of North Carolina is known for its unique pocosin habitat. It is remote and nearly impenetrable, access being mostly by the sounds and rivers surrounding the refuge.[3] Here the warm season is only occasionally long enough to provide a suitable environment for sustained regeneration of alligators.

Another habitat suitable for alligators, the Burns, is a large wetland area south of Lake Charles, Louisiana, deep in the heart of the region where Cajun culture and zydeco music flourish. Situated east of State Highway 27, south of the Intracoastal Waterway, west of the Mermentau River, and north of the Little Chenier ridge road, this vast wetland is a great field of fine green plant life broken only by the water trails and parted by boats carrying people who fish and hunt. The sky over the Burns meets the water in a refined definition of the horizon. When a storm moves in, visible from a distance, the quiet vanishes as a threatening sheet of wind and water sweeps across the surface. Once the storm passes, the landscape is a soft, pearlescent green in the sunlight.

The region where the Guadalupe and San Antonio Rivers converge and run into San Antonio Bay along State Highway 35 just north of Tivoli, Texas, is wooded and marshy low country. This bayou and river habitat of the Guadalupe delta is rife with alligators. On riverbanks and along shorelines you may find footprints and tracks where an alligator has dragged its tail, perhaps alerting a hunter or naturalist to its imminent presence.

Hunting is allowed seasonally in Louisiana, Florida, Texas, and most recently in South Carolina. These states have alligator management programs based on the concept of value-added conservation, which asserts that if an animal has some economic value, that value can contribute to the conservation of the species.

Both Louisiana's and Florida's management agencies initially established experimental alligator harvest programs. The Louisiana Department of Wildlife and Fisheries began its study in 1972, and the Florida Game and Fresh Water Fish Commission did so in 1981. The purpose of the studies was to determine what percentage of wild alligators could be harvested without depleting the population, recognizing alligators as an ecologically, aesthetically, and economically valuable resource.[4] Beginning in 1984, Florida took applications for controlled alligator hunts, and a statewide managed hunt was established in 1988. Alligator agent-trapper applicants entered a lottery for the limited licenses available during the experimental hunts. The rules for hunting were specific; the application notices emphasized the importance of gathering biological data from each animal taken and measuring the effort hunters ex-pended during the hunt. The agency stressed a cooperative working relationship between the hunters, the biologists, and management personnel. As a result of these studies, the state of Florida opened an annual alligator hunting season in fall 1988. Texas had authorized a regulated hunt in 1984, and Louisiana did so statewide as early as 1981.[5]

In 1995 South Carolina authorized a seasonal hunt limited to private lands comprising one hundred acres or more—big abandoned rice plantations and their managed tidal wetlands that are privately

owned. South Carolina's hunts, also based on sustained yield harvest allotments projected from surveys, are aimed at adding value to the alligators' habitat so owners will be encouraged to manage the wetlands effectively.

There are numerous protected areas for alligators in the southern United States. Federal, state, and privately supported reserves of alligator habitat are maintained from Florida to as far west as the eastern Texas–Mexico border and eastern Oklahoma and as far north as North Carolina. Florida and Louisiana have the most abundant populations, and their state regulations allow different uses of available alligator resources. Besides protected areas for wild alligators, Alabama, Florida, Georgia, Louisiana, Mississippi, and Texas have ranching and farming. In Georgia the Okefenokee National Wildlife Refuge and the Okefenokee Swamp Park are two huge adjoining conservation areas where alligators thrive. The Okefenokee, with its "trembling earth"— islands of floating peat and blackwater— is a provocative environment, inspiring local professionals such as "busy lumberman" Hamp Mizell and "country lawyer" A. S. McQueen to collaborate on a colorfully written illustrated history of the swamp and songwriter Okefenokee Joe to compose lyrics about mosquitoes, snapping turtles, big bull gators, and black bears in affectionate terms.[6]

For more than a century now, inspired thinkers like John Wesley Powell, Theodore Roosevelt, Archie Carr, Rachel Carson, and Aldo Leopold have articulated the idea that it is possible for all animals to live in concert while sustaining their populations and environments. At the top of the food chain, humans bear the responsibility of consciously managing their own activities to guarantee a balance between development and maintenance of the ecosystem. The relationship between people and alligators illustrates this responsibility. We are fascinated with the primordial semblance of alligators, and, in a few cases when alligators have harmed humans and their pets, we all vicariously feel threatened.

Alligators are challenging to hunt and profitable to ranch and farm. Their interesting life history has only recently been researched and comprehensively understood. With the resurgence of alligator populations throughout the southern wetlands, we have another chance to provide for the coexistence of humans and alligators in the environment.

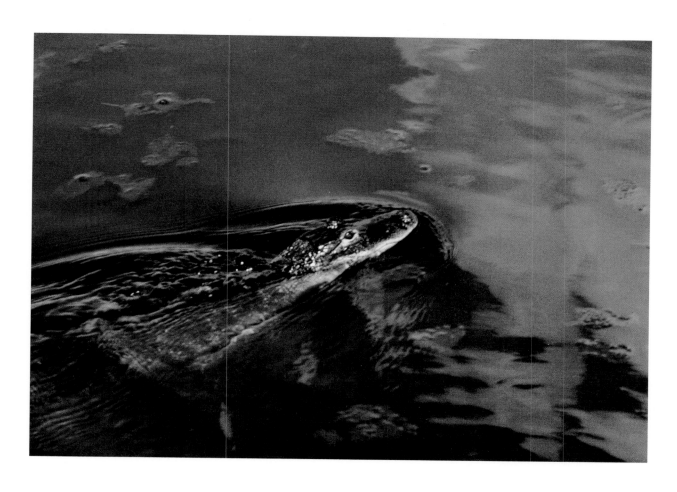

Mysterious Crocodilia

The words crocodilia and crocodile are derived from the Greek *krokodilos*, "gravel worm," applied since Herodotus, the fifth-century B.C. Greek historian, to the giant reptiles of the Nile. Since then the word has taken many forms, leading to confusion that has included association with an imaginary reptilian bird-beast that picks the crocodile's teeth, a water snake born from a cock's egg that kills by its mere glance, and the notion that the crocodile moans to attract its victims and sheds tears while devouring them. As members of the order Crocodilia, alligators inherit the same connotations.[7]

Alligator comes from the Latin word *lacertus*, "upper arm," also used for lizards, which the Romans associated with the shape and size of an arm. The Spanish word for lizard is *el lagarto*, which in the New World was transcribed by several English spellings, including alligator, alligarter, and allegator.

Symbolically, crocodilians blend different aspects, representing the influence of two of the various elements—earth, fire, wind, and water. Because of their perceived viciousness and destructive strength, crocodilians came to signify fury and evil in Egyptian hieroglyphics. Also, since they inhabit both earth and water and are associated with mud and vegetation, they became emblems of fecundity and power. Because of their resemblance to dragons and serpents, they are also symbols of knowledge. In Egyptian history the dead were portrayed as transformed into crocodiles of knowledge, an idea linked with the zodiacal sign we know as Capricorn. Crocodilians also represent death and rebirth through the inversion principle. As explained in *A Dictionary of Symbols*, "The continuity of life is assured by the mutual sacrifice which is consummated on the peak of the mystic mountain: death permits rebirth; all opposites are for an instant

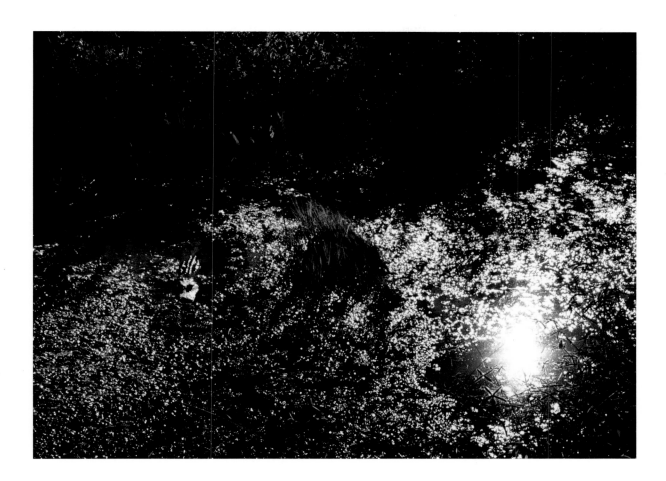

fused together and then inverted."[8] The association of crocodilians with death or sacrifice therefore represents rebirth. These ideas and beliefs, with their powerful connotations, have been passed down in the Occident through centuries of mythological and spiritual teachings. As we approach alligators, our general perceptions are colored by these teachings.

At present we are fascinated and awed by alligators. They stimulate our imaginations because they represent their predecessors in appearance and life history. When scientists give information on dinosaurs, they frequently compare them to

alligators, as in an *Omni* magazine article titled "The Biggest Carnivore of All?" and in a *New Yorker* essay, "The Dinosaur Heretic."[9] In both instances our knowledge of present-day alligators in their primordial habitats is used to inform us about dinosaurs.

Walking on a slatted boardwalk just a couple of feet above the water in the Okefenokee Swamp or the Everglades, we are in close proximity to the fauna and flora. We feel we are in the same environment as the wetland creatures around us. The light glistening on the blackwater meets our eyes as it fractures and reflects

on leaves, grasses, and the scutes of an alligator's partially submerged back. The image of contrasting dark and bright, stillness and movement projects a deceiving impression. The wet habitat steams in the heat. If the alligator perceives much intrusion, it drops slowly into its dark, wet underwater realm. Only a bubble trail may give away its location, but even that is ambiguous, since gases from the peat or bubbles made by other animals may camouflage its presence. This primordial home of the alligator is a lush, alluring place for people as well.

Wetlands and Deepwaters

As mysterious and dramatic as the sparkle of light on the blackwater—made dark by tannin produced by bottom sediment of decaying leaves, berries, bark, and roots of vegetation such as cypress, oak, bay, maple, and gum trees, cattails, and saw grass—American alligators float secretively in waterways throughout the southern wetlands and deepwaters. Areas where they have thrived for thousands of years include Paynes Prairie, a vast 20,000 acre preserve managed by the Florida Park Service, south of Gainesville, Florida, off U.S. 441. Among the most significant natural and historical areas in Florida, the preserve's main geological feature is the prairie basin, formed thousands of years ago as the underlying limestone dissolved, causing subsequent settling of the terrain.[10] The park is a prime preserve for wildlife, a recreation area for birders and wildlife enthusiasts, and a research laboratory for scientists.

As mysterious as the alligator is Tate's Hell (see page 29), described by the late Will McLean, known as Florida's Troubadour, who wrote and sang about the state's history, legends, and mysteries for more than thirty years. Tate's Hell swamp is just west of Carrabelle up toward Sumatra. Will's lyrics are:

Oh, listen, good people!
A story I'll tell
Of a great swamp in Florida,
A place called "Tate's Hell,"
One hundred and forty
Square watery miles
With millions of 'skeeters
And big yellow flies;

And where all about
The moccasins lie,
With glittering death
In their beady eye;

Where bull-gators beller
And panthers squall.
Now this is a place
To be shunned by all![11]

This environmentally sensitive habitat was recently purchased for preservation by the state of Florida. Money for this acquisition came from the CARL (Conservation and Recreational Lands) fund. Conservation of diverse habitats is offering another form of "collecting" to patrons interested in preserving and enhancing our quality of life environmentally. Like other collections of precious things, collecting habitats by public and private means encourages their maintenance and endurance. It constitutes stewardship.

As human population increases in and around areas where alligators live, there is obvious concern for development and loss of habitat. Likewise, there is great potential for people to appreciate the need to coexist with other creatures that inspire our imaginations and are critical to the health of the biotic cycle in which people participate.

The Everglades in south Florida are perhaps the most symbolic of wetlands because of their uniqueness and the long struggle to preserve them. This wetland was called a "river of grass" by Marjory Stoneman Douglas in her 1947 book of that name. The Seminoles called it Pay-haio-kee, "grassy water." White people named it "Ever Glade."

The Everglades lie in a shallow trough from thirty to sixty miles wide, extending from Lake Okeechobee to the southern tip of Florida. On the east a narrow coastal ridge rises to a maximum of about thirty feet above sea level, separating the Everglades from a series of coastal bays, the largest being Biscayne Bay in the vicinity of Miami and Lake Worth near Palm Beach. On the west a wide sandy area of slightly higher ground separates the Everglades from the Gulf of Mexico and embraces the areas known as the Devil's Garden and Big Cypress Swamp. The bottom of the trough slopes from about fourteen to twenty feet above mean sea level near Lake Okeechobee to tide level at its south end, about a hundred miles away. This is the current configuration of the Everglades. Peninsular Florida has been under the sea a number of times: As recently as ten thousand years ago Lake Okeechobee was a shallow depression in the sea floor. Both natural changes and those resulting from human development have altered this region.[12]

American Indians were the first known inhabitants of south Florida. They lived along the shores of this huge water system, changing the surface only slightly by digging canals for navigational and ceremonial purposes. The Spaniards followed. Florida was opened for development by Ponce de León in 1513 as he journeyed in search of the Fountain of Youth. The first non-native slave in America may have been Escalante de Fontaneda, who was enslaved by the Calusa Indians between 1551 and 1566 after surviving a shipwreck. Fontaneda was told about a giant freshwater lake called Mayaimi where there were many Indian communities. This was Lake Okeechobee, as named later by the Seminoles, meaning "big water." There is no evidence that Florida's early immigrants attempted any water control.

The history of Florida's water control began with the inception of statehood. West Florida was occupied in 1813 as part of the Louisiana Purchase; East Florida was still Spanish in 1818 when it was invaded by General Andrew Jackson, and it became a United States territory in 1822. In 1845 the region became the state of Florida with the condition that the state never interfere with the primary disposal of the public lands lying within it. The potential importance of that large body of federally owned swamplands known as the Everglades was recognized by the officials of the newly created state, and they moved to reclaim them. In 1847 one of the state's original senators, J. D. Westcott, made the first known proposal to drain the overflowed lands of the lower peninsula.

Though Westcott's proposal never became law, the United States Congress passed what is generally referred to as the Swamp and Overflowed Lands Grant Act on 28 September 1850, granting each state of the Union those swamp and overflowed lands within its boundaries that remained unsold by the federal government at that time. It enabled the states

army engineers to draft a new plan for constructing floodway channels, control gates, and major levees along Okeechobee's shores. Though these plans were once thought to be only of local concern, what has emerged is the interrelation of water systems: A basic difficulty began to assert itself as the complex nature of the region was revealed.

Successive dry spells from 1931 through 1945 brought to light an important connection between the areas around Lake Okeechobee and the other water resources of the region that had been overlooked in earlier efforts to drain the interior. When the water level fell in the Everglades, salt water from the ocean rose in the wells that supplied the cities. Also, land that was regularly flooded dried out and shrank visibly. Fires started and the peaty muckland base was consumed, to be regained only over centuries, if at all. Then, as Florida survived the Depression and entered the expansion period after World War II, a great strain was placed on its other resources. More water and land were needed, which is still the problem, though the state has been addressing it for nearly half a century. Nature has been disrupted, and county and city governments have planned insufficiently to restore the balance.

In 1947 the Everglades National Park was established. Biologists and park managers have worked with state and federal agencies to identify and rectify the water problems in concert with meeting human needs. Not only is the correct flow of water an issue, but pollution is as well. An experimental project to deliver water to the Everglades National Park is

"to construct the necessary levees and drains to reclaim the swamp and overflowed lands therein." Florida acquired twenty million acres, including the Everglades. An important stipulation was that the sale of the lands to private interests should finance the necessary reclamation work. Thus began the history of water control in Florida, which has included early private drainage development by Hamilton Disston, twentieth-century federal drainage spurred by the United States Army Corps of Engineers' examination and survey of the Kissimmee-Okeechobee-Caloosahatchee system, and

then further state and federal projects.

The idea behind the drainage movement was that the reclaimed areas would be the best cultivated land in the Union. Followers believed drainage would ensure a new agricultural empire in south Florida. They were right, but at what cost?

In 1926 and again in 1928, hurricanes ravaged Florida, sweeping across Lake Okeechobee. The wind-driven waters, augmented by torrential rains, overflowed the lakeshore and drowned thousands of people. There was vast destruction of property twice in these two years. In 1928 President Herbert Hoover authorized

now being considered. In effect, the Army Corps of Engineers is proposing to undo what was done, mostly between 1948 and 1971, when it completed a century-old effort to drain and tame the Everglades ecosystem. The current proposal is not based on traditional economic justification, because no traditional economic benefit is expected. Therefore the proposed action necessitates an exemption for a specially authorized project.[13]

The problems of the south Florida aquatic lands are numerous and complex. Human greed is definitely in play, and we still lack knowledge about the physical system itself. As the pendulum swings, informed human concern and stewardship are also important parts of the picture as humans and alligators share environments. Education of the public is significant in any future scenario. People need a sustainable habitat; ultimately, theirs is not so different from that needed by other animals.

Alligator Management

As airboats cut swaths through the grasses along the shore of Lake Okeechobee and in the Everglades, they leave channels of parted vegetation that are reused by fishers, hunters, sightseers, management personnel, and ecotourists. Except for the channels and the noise they create, airboats are considered the machines least damaging to the wildlife in wetlands and deepwater habitats because their propellers do minimal damage to the flora and the fauna. Butch, a dog that sights water animals, has slash marks left by boat propellers on his many forays into the waters of Florida to chase ducks, marsh hens, or alligators. The hunter will become the hunted if the gator is big enough, and there are enough alligators in southern waters to threaten animals and people who do not know or observe safety precautions. Thus most counties inhabited by alligators in southern states have nuisance alligator control programs and personnel.

On 11 July 1993, LeRoy Overstreet caught an alligator at daybreak in Willard Tucker's pond, between Sweet Water and Dixons Mills, Alabama. The ten foot, seven inch alligator had been taking fish from Mr. Tucker's stocked trout pond and

scaring away his fishing clients. LeRoy is a nuisance control hunter for errant alligators in Pickens, Sumter, Greene, Marengo, Tuscaloosa, and Choctaw Counties. On this Sunday morning more than one hundred people had come from miles around to watch and take part in this rather unusual event in the Alabama pasturelands. Willard Tucker responded by cutting into a truckload of watermelons while Mrs. Tucker served coffee to all those who came to watch the capture, view the alligator's carcass, visit, and eat watermelons before going to church or to the car races later in the day.

Nuisance calls are common in southern states in the summer months. As these instances increase, the issues related to ecological balance become more obvious. State agents work to identify and resolve problems through research programs carried out in numerous aquatic preserves, and on public and private lands. Alligators are caught, marked, and released to be monitored through recapture and comparative study over years of growth.

Phil Wilkinson, a noted alligator and waterfowl research biologist, was the wildlife staff member Tom Yawkey employed in the late 1960s to develop a re-

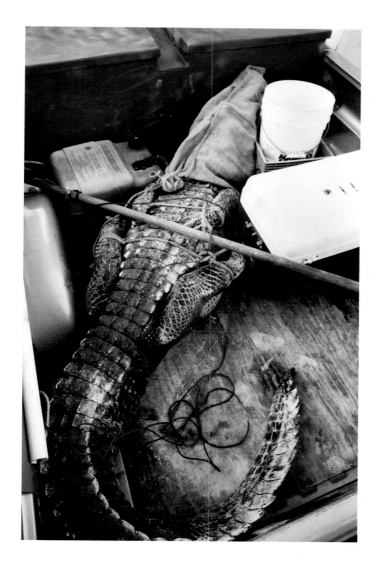

search and management program for his private lands, South Island Plantation in South Carolina. Wilkinson encouraged Yawkey to explore new ways of improving wildlife habitat and to endow a preserve on his death. South Carolina inherited the preserve, considered to be one of the most outstanding gifts to conservation in North America, and the money to ensure biological expertise in managing those wetlands, just south of Georgetown.[14]

The job of management and research personnel from centers like Yawkey's thereafter becomes education. Many people who have lived in wetlands understand the ways of mutual existence in an ecosystem where humans and alligators thrive. But with the influx of new people unfamiliar with wetlands life, harmonious ecological coexistence becomes threatened.

When alligators threaten stock, pets, or people, they are either captured and moved or destroyed. Removing and translocating alligators is difficult to manage effectively because of their powerful homing instinct. Thus they must be moved thirty miles or more to translocate them successfully. There is no need to restock alligators, and it would be unwise to place bold, conditioned animals, acclimated to people, in wilderness areas where they might attack unwary canoeists or kayakers. When a problem alligator is captured by a nuisance control trapper, most commonly it is destroyed, especially when there are many complaints. At the time of capture trappers are required to record the alligator's location, size, and sex and report to the state, along with specific information about the marketing of its skin and meat. Occasionally trappers and processors are also asked to collect specimens for scientific research.

Destruction
Out of meanness or for the challenge of killing a descendent of the dinosaurs, people sometimes wantonly destroy alligators, leaving their meat and skin to rot. The wild and scenic Wakulla River in northern Florida is a nature preserve where alligator hunting is illegal.

Animals and Habitat

Alligator habitat is diverse. Alligators are found in freshwater marshes and swamps, lakes and ponds, rivers, bayous, brackish estuaries, and saltwater coastal marshes and backwaters. Their population is most evident at night when beams of light flash back and forth across the dark swamps or lake waters, producing double reflections.

Eyeshine

Alligator eyeshine is distinct. One glowing ember sits directly above another; on top is the light reflected from the eye, and below is the eye's reflection in the water. E. A. McIlhenny writes that the "eyes of the adult males shine red, and the eyes of the females and young a greenish or bluish yellow."[15] It is now thought that the size of the alligator and the intensity of the light may be responsible for the different colors. Alligators' eyes are large, and their eyeshine can be seen for two to three hundred yards with powerful spotlights. In the evening landscape, each pair of reflections represents an alligator.

In conducting population counts, eyeshine is used to count animals during night light surveys. In both Florida and Louisiana, the alligator population has revived enough to permit hunting, trapping, harvesting, and ranching programs in which eggs produced in the wild are hatched and reared in captivity. It has also grown enough to necessitate nuisance capture programs and to expand intensive life history, management, and marketing research.

Memories of
GATOR HUNTS

I can't remember the first time I went alligator hunting—that first time just didn't leave a memory with me. I wanted to start out this story by describing the thrill of my first hunt, but since I can't remember, I will tell about my first really hair-raising experience with an alligator.

I was probably eight or nine years old. We lived a few miles out from Haines City, Florida, at the time. North of our house about a quarter mile was a huge marsh covered with water about waist deep. Cattails, water lilies, and flags grew in the water so thick you had to work real hard to pole a frog boat through it. A grove of banana trees grew all along the edge of the marsh.

My father had cleared the land adjoining the banana trees. All kinds of wildlife lived in the banana grove and the shallow-water marsh. There were swamp rabbits, otters, alligators, and plenty of snakes and turtles. I used to enjoy exploring the grove to discover and observe the wildlife. I never was scared of snakes, but my father had taught me a healthy respect for them. He also taught me how to part the grass and weeds with a stick and how to spot a snake by looking carefully before you took each step.

A snake is usually as scared of you as you are of it, and it will almost always run away from you if you give it the chance. The only snakes we really worried about were the rattlesnake and the cottonmouth moccasin. The rattlesnakes would make their rattles sing when they felt threatened. The cottonmouth moccasin would lie coiled up, and when it felt threatened it would open its mouth wide and prepare to strike. The cottonmouth is a rather short, stubby snake, colored a dark brown on its back. When it would lie with its mouth open and look up at you, the inside was as white as cotton.

I was slipping through the weeds, parting them with a stick and watching for old Cotton Mouth when I noticed a mound of fresh brown muck and brown flags and grass that I couldn't recall ever seeing before. My curiosity was aroused. I went over to the mound and lifted up the top, and there lay about a bucketful of large white eggs. About the time I saw the eggs, I heard a noise behind me that sounded like a porpoise blowing. I looked around and there, coming straight at me with her mouth open wide enough to drive a truck in, was the biggest gator that I had ever seen in my life!

Now a gator is a reptile, and one of the factors that has helped it survive since the age of the dinosaurs is the fact that the mama gator guards her nest and watches over her eggs and young better than any setting hen. She will attack anything she thinks even remotely threatens her eggs or young.

I ran as fast as I could toward the banana trees with the gator right behind me, gaining on me with every step. Her jaws popping together sounded like a door slamming. I reached the first banana tree just ahead of the gator and climbed right up it like it had stairs. A banana tree will grow up from the ground in a matter of a few weeks. It will bear fruit and then fall over to rot and fertilize future generations of banana trees. The outside of the tree becomes as slick as goose grease, and the tree can be easily pushed over.

I had climbed up about ten or twelve feet and I was slipping back down, so I made a desperate effort and managed to get my hands into the base of the leaves. Just as I thought I might be safe, the tree started falling over. I didn't wait for it to hit the ground. I jumped and hit the ground running as fast as I could, with the gator right behind me. I ran to another banana tree and climbed it, and the same thing happened. On my way down I spotted a myrtle bush with limbs about as big around as my arm. It was my only hope, so I scrambled up into it, about six or seven feet off the ground, as high as I could get.

I spent the rest of the afternoon begging for somebody to please come help me.

Finally, when no help came, I gave up and resigned myself to the fact that the gator was going to knock the myrtle bush down and eat me and there was nothing I could do about it. I got real quiet and still, and after another hour of wallowing around, blowing and popping her jaws, the gator finally left. I felt great relief, and this experience taught me to conquer fear and rely on my own ability to extricate myself from future messy situations.

Later I went back to show the nest to my granddad; the mama gator wasn't around. We counted the eggs as best we could without disturbing them, and there appeared to be about fifty.

Hunting gators provided a livelihood for a lot of Crackers who didn't have any other way to make a living. The valuable part of the gator is its hide—it makes beautiful and durable luggage, purses, boots, shoes, and many other products. The gator has a hard, almost bulletproof shell on its back and the top of its head and tail. This part has no value, so the only parts you skin are the belly, legs, and underside of the tail.

The hide buyers paid for the hides by the foot. The first hides I remember selling brought twenty-five cents a foot if they had buttons and fifty cents a foot if they didn't. Buttons are the places on the belly where the hide has turned to shell or bone. These places have to be cut out of the hide, so they drastically reduce the value. Female gators start getting buttons when they

3 4

LeRoy Overstreet

Memories

of Gator Hunts

get to nine or ten feet long. Males are usually free of buttons until about twelve feet, but I have killed males fourteen feet long that didn't have any.

The buyer would lay the hide out and measure it: If it measured nine feet, eleven inches, you only got paid for nine feet. Consequently we tried to stretch the hide as much as possible to make it fall into the next longer bracket. We rolled it up after we had salted it, stretching the roll as tight as possible and tying the rolled-up hide with string. We could also gain an inch or so by skinning all the way up over the bottom jaw to the teeth.

I don't know how much gator hunting contributed to the central Florida economy, but for me and many more of us it provided most of our income. Tourism was supposed to be the major contribution to the economy. Once a tourist asked Eddie Seaver how he made his living. Eddie said that he skinned gators all summer and Yankees all winter.

When I first started hunting gators, there was no law against using both a light and a gun. I left Kissimmee one Sunday night right after dark and poled a boat, hunting gators all the way around the shoreline of Lake Tohopekaliga. The trip took till the following Sunday morning; I would hunt all night and sleep in the daytime.

I took some canned goods with me and a box of biscuits. I used a six-volt automobile storage battery to burn my headlight. The light was still bright after six nights of hunting. I took a piece of canvas in case it rained and a five-gallon lard can about half full of salt to salt the hides. I killed a rabbit almost every night and hung it by the fire to cook while I was skinning the night's catch of gators.

I killed several on this trip that were too big to load in the boat, so I pulled them up in shallow water as far as I could and skinned them on the spot.

The greatest woodsman I ever knew, and the man that taught me how to hunt, was Rossie Clemens. He wasn't quite as good a rifle shot as his brother Raymond, but he was a much better woodsman and understood wild critters better. It was uncanny how Raymond could shoot a .22 rifle. He could hit running squirrels every shot and always shot them in the head. The .22 was our only weapon; the cartridges for any other caliber would have been too expensive for us. Very few people had motors, and we poled, rowed, or paddled our boats wherever we went.

Rossie taught me how to stalk a gator and get in position to shoot it. The gator must be killed instantly with one shot, or it would sink and we would lose it. Rossie taught me never to approach a gator from the front, since it was almost impossible to make a sure killing shot on account of the hard plate that covered the head. If you approached from any other direction than straight ahead, there was a soft spot from the eye all the way around the back

▮▮▮ The Hunt

The hunt begins in the late afternoon when the sun drops low in the sky and the air cools, the time some say is best for hunting. As boats move out, hunters can see alligators emerge from underwater into the twilight. Between dusk and nightfall the hunters take a break, talking softly as the swamp noises permeate the air. At dark the hunt resumes. Headbeams sweep across the aquatic environment in great arcs seeking the reflected eyeshine. The sounds of airboats and motorboats slowly searching are heard across the water, yet not as persistently as the buzzing of mosquitoes in the swamp night. Then a gunned engine resounds, a beam holds steady in the dark, and the hunter moves in on the prey.

of the head to the other eye. The trick was to place the bullet so it would enter the soft spot and then travel on to the center of the spine or brain. The gator would die instantly. It would not exhale and would stay afloat and give you plenty of time to drag it over the side into the boat.

The biggest gator I ever killed like this was more than sixteen feet long and weighed close to a ton. All the folks that hunted with me used nothing but a .22 rifle. The Garrett brothers from over in Polk County used a 45-70 Springfield military rifle that would penetrate the gator's hide anywhere on its body. It kicked like a mule, and one cartridge for it cost almost as much as a whole box of .22 shells, but they had a very lucrative business catching little gators and stuffing them to sell to the Yankees. They would make lamps and all kinds of conversation pieces with them. They had a stuffed gator in the middle of their taxidermy shop that was eighteen feet long and about four or five feet around its belly. It was supposed to be the largest gator ever killed.

When you shined your light around the lake or marsh, the gator's eyes would reflect the light and look bright red. You could see its eyes for a hundred yards or more. After you located the gator, you just had to pole the boat up to it silently without letting the pole bump the boat. Any sharp noise and the gator would sink. When stalking you must never shine the light directly on the gator until you were ready to shoot or it would sink. You'd use just enough of the edge of the light to make the eyes shine dimly so you could keep it located.

In case the gator did sink, Rossie taught me how to make the grunting noises small gators use to call their mothers. Most times the grunts would make the gator come back up, and you could get a shot at it.

In the spring during mating season the male gators would bellow with a noise that could be heard for several miles. Other gators would hear and answer, and when a whole marshful of gators started bellowing it would make your hair stand up. The sound they made was something like the low note of a ship's foghorn, except it kind of rumbled and the pitch would start out low, rise, and then fall.

I found a hummock in a marsh once where the gators were bellowing and had wallowed the grass down over a considerable area. I poled my frog boat out there and hid in a flag pond real close to the hummock one moonlit night, hoping I could see what went on there. Shortly after dark, a gator crawled out of the water and stood up on his hind legs with his body vertical, tipped his head forward until it was horizontal, and started to bellow. Very shortly, he was joined by several other large gators, and they were bellowing and fighting and thrashing around all over the hummock. It was a sight to behold! I was fascinated and watched them carry on for about three hours. When I left, they were still at it.

With the recent return of alligators in large numbers, people living near wetlands, rivers, and lakes were able to resume gator hunting to supplement their incomes. Harvesting alligators provides an economic incentive to save wetlands and deepwater habitats and preserves a way of life for southerners who traditionally have hunted and processed these animals. Alligator harvesting can contribute one-third or more of the annual income of hunter households. Gator hunting is also a way of life that contributes to cultural identity and a sense of community.

There are numerous methods of capturing and hunting alligators. Some hunters set live traps, hooks, or snares or use harpoons, gigs, snatch hooks, and manual spears, spear guns, crossbows, or bows with projectiles attached to a restraining line; others use fire power, such as firearms, or "bang sticks."

Larry Cameron of South Carolina recalls Will Alston's description of how to trap an alligator alive, Low Country style: "You drag a dead goat through the marsh, smearing its blood as you go. As you drag the goat to higher ground, you put in a curved path bordered by zigzag cedar stakes, and you place the goat at the end of the curve. Then you wait for the gator to make his way up the entwining trail to the bait. Once there the trapped animal is bordered by stakes curving the length of its body, and can be captured alive."[16]

Gators build themselves caves in the marshes and swamps by rooting up the lily pad roots and fanning out big holes. They take the muck, roots, and vegetation to one side and pile it up in a hummock. This hummock will grow a quick crop of marsh grasses and weeds that stabilizes it. The gator will keep adding to it until the hummock is a few feet above the water level, then the gator will dig a cave from the pond it has made up into the hummock so that the cave has an air space in it. It will build a shelf in the cave to store food on, and it will hibernate there during the winter.

Gators do not like fresh meat. I have opened caves that had birds, rabbits, fish, and turtles lying on the food shelf in various stages of decay. A gator will hardly ever eat a freshly killed meal. Rather, food will be stored on the food shelf until it spoils enough to suit the gator's palate. Then it is mealtime.

During periods of drought, the fish, turtles, and other wildlife gather at the gator holes because they contain the only water left. The gator will lie around and get fat, since meals are plentiful then.

It is interesting to sit and watch a gator lie up real close to the bank and imitate a log. A rabbit, coon, or some other animal will come to the bank and step out on the log to get a drink. The instant the animal steps off its back, the gator explodes into action and catches the animal, faster than the eye can follow. I have never seen one miss. I have seen rabbits walk from one end of the log to the other and drink and wash several times. The gator always lies perfectly still until the instant the animal leaves its back.

This trait is well known to all woodsmen who work around gators. We were always taught to drag our feet when wading. If you kick a gator in the side it will swim off, but if you step on its back it will catch you every time just as you take your foot off.

A group of us were pulling a pocket seine in Lake Kissimmee once, before the lake was closed to seining. The net was 1,500 yards long and had a pocket near one end that would hold several tons of fish. The net was tied to a post at the pocket end, the wing was stretched out in a big circle, and we were pulling it around to come back by the post to close the pocket. One of the men stepped on a gator's back—I can't recall his name. All of us were barefooted, so he knew he must not take his foot off till help arrived.

He hollered and told us what had happened, and we all dropped the net and went to his aid. The water was about four feet deep. We had two large seine boats, one to carry the net and the other for the fish. Five of us got in one boat and five got in the other. We positioned the boats on either side of the man, and two men held the boats together at the proper distance while two men in each boat took hold of him by the armpits. On the count of three we hoisted him straight up with all our strength.

We weren't fast enough. The gator caught the man's leg, and we had a tug-of-war with the gator twisting round and round until he finally came loose. The man's leg was mangled horribly, and for a long time the doctors were afraid he might lose it.

The gator had laid there all that time without so much as a twitch—more than twenty minutes. It did not move until the instant the foot left its back.

When I was about seventeen I got interested in rodeos and left Florida to perform all over the United States, Canada, and Mexico. I only came home occasionally, and I didn't get back into serious gator hunting until the late 1940s. By then it was a whole new ball game. We had to be licensed. We could not have a gun and a light together in a boat anymore. The penalty if you were caught was five hundred dollars, and they would confiscate all your equipment (boat, motor, truck, trailer, and anything else you had with you at the time). But being wise in the ways of gators, it didn't take us long to develop legal ways to catch them.

One of the best ways was to capitalize on the gators' fondness for spoiled meat or fish. We would take five-gallon lard cans and fill them with mud fish or mullet that weighed about two pounds each. We'd close the cans and leave them sitting out in the sun for three or four days until the fish was thoroughly rotten and smelled to high heaven. It took a strong stomach and the courage of a lion to open the lid of one of those cans. I've seen big, strapping men incapacitated by just one whiff of gator bait. But it smelled like ambrosia to a gator. I have watched them swimming around downwind from where I was baiting a hook, getting closer and closer to that delicious aroma. I've seen them take my fresh-set bait in broad daylight before I could get more than a hundred yards away. If the gator came by and smelled it, it couldn't resist.

We would use a piece of three-eighths-inch grass rope about twenty-five feet long with a fourteen-aught O'Shaughnessy shark hook braided onto one end. We would work the hook gently down through the putrid fish from the tail so the hook would be completely buried with its point near the head. Then we would tie the loose end of the rope to a stout stake or tree on the shore. We'd tie the baited hook to a limb hanging out over the water by a piece of cotton twine. The bait would hang about a foot above the water, out of reach of a small gator. The gator had to be six feet long or over to be legal. The gator would take the bait, and when it pulled down the twine would break so it could swallow the bait whole. The gator eats only rotten food, which is soft. It doesn't do any chewing at all. Its teeth are rounded, with wide spaces between them. The only thing the gator uses its teeth for is to kill prey. The rope would lie between its rounded teeth with no danger they'd cut it.

I had a custom-made commercial fishing boat that was fast, was very seaworthy, and could carry a heavy load. This type of boat was known as a skipjack. I had a ten-horsepower Wizard motor (we called it a kicker) that would push it about twenty-five miles an hour. I also had a van to pull it around that was fixed up so two people could sleep in it.

I heard about a plan the Game and Fish Commission had, to spray the water hyacinths in Walk-in-Water Creek to kill them. The creek had been stopped up with hyacinths for years. It meandered through a large, wide swamp, all the way from Walk-in-Water Lake to Lake Rosalie, about fifty miles following the creek. I knew the creek would be full of gators because nobody had been able to get to them for years. I recruited Buddy Lunsford to help me. He would pay half the expenses, help with skinning and all, and get half the profits.

We checked the creek regularly, and as soon as the dead hyacinths started moving into Lake Rosalie with the current we decided it was time to start. We loaded up a big commercial fishing icebox and four or five stout cane poles about fourteen feet long and went to Titusville to catch bait. We rigged the poles with a strong piece of line about ten feet long and tied on a 4-0 treble hook with the barbs filed off. We took up a position under a railroad bridge where the water ran real fast when the tide turned. It was just after dark, and we didn't have long to wait until the tide started rushing through and we commenced trolling our barbless and baitless hooks through the rushing water.

In just a few minutes I was catching more mullet than Buddy could pick up in his five-gallon buckets and carry to the icebox. I'd whip the hook out, pull it back toward me, snag a fish, and flip it over my head onto the bank, where the fish would flop off. Then I'd repeat the maneuver so I was catching a mullet about every three seconds. Before the mullet quit running, we'd caught the icebox full of fish that weighed about two pounds each.

We felt so good that we split open a couple and cooked them in their scales over the coals of the fire we'd built while we were waiting for the tide to turn.

When we got back home, we filled five five-gallon lard cans with mullet and set them out in the sun. After three or four days Buddy and I decided to open one of the cans to check on the bait. When I opened the lid the fumes knocked Buddy flat on his back and seared the grass brown for a hundred yards downwind. I pronounced the bait ready, and just before daylight the next morning we parked Buddy's car where the Highway 60 bridge crossed Walk-in-Water Creek about halfway between Walk-in-Water Lake and Lake Rosalie. We both got in the van and drove on down to the south end of Walk-in-Water Lake, where we launched the boat. We set hooks in all the likely places around the east side of the lake until we came to the creek, then started setting hooks down the creek.

After we got three or four miles into the creek, we began to run into tremendous jams of water hyacinths. The motor was useless: The roots would wind up in the propeller so it wouldn't provide any push. Buddy got in the bow on his knees and cut through the vegetation as far as he could reach with an oar. I'd stand up on the back seat with the pole and push with all my strength. We struggled through the creek like this all day long, and sometime

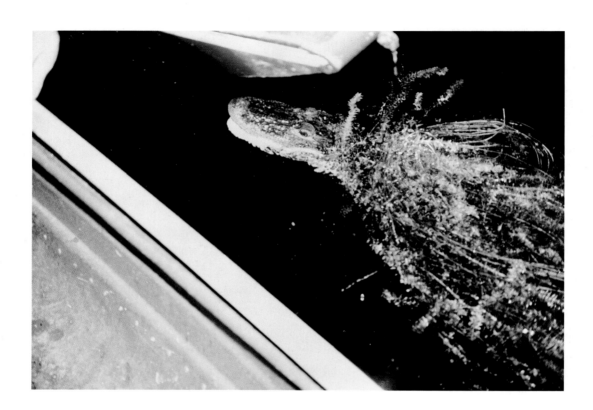

"BANG STICK," ORANGE LAKE, FLORIDA, SEPTEMBER 1987

A bang stick is a rod with an impact-activated cartridge mounted at the end. When an alligator is pulled to the edge of the boat on a harpoon cable, the hunter knocks the end of the bang stick into its head, discharging the shell and killing the gator instantly. The bang stick is the preferred method of dispatching because it eliminates injured animals' escaping.

The most common method used by hunters today is to locate the gator by its eyeshine, harpoon it, kill it with a bang stick, sever the spinal cord, and haul the animal into the boat. The most dangerous part of hunting is grabbing the animal

and hoisting it aboard. First the gator is pulled partially out of the water onto the gunnel, then a hatchet is used to sever both the spinal cord and the brain stem, disabling the gator's reflexes so it cannot bite or swipe its tail at the hunter. Then the animal can be safely loaded. Alligators of various lengths, as they are caught, are stored in the boat until the return to shore.

Alligator hunters share an awareness of danger on the water. They must be keenly alert and mindful of the animal's power and its habits. Once an alligator closes its jaws on a limb, the force is so great that it is virtually impossible for a human to open them again.[17] The swipe of an alligator's tail can knock a person into the water, where the animal is most agile, powerful, and potentially destructive.

after dark two very tired young gator hunters made it to the bridge. We tied up the boat, piled into the van, drove to Buddy's car, and took both vehicles and the boat trailer home.

The next morning we left the van and trailer at Lake Rosalie and spent the day on the rest of the creek. We were even more tired when we got back to Lake Rosalie than we were the night before. We had set about eighty hooks.

The next day we started running the hooks. We had a boatload of gators by the time we got to the bridge, so we hid them in the swamp and ran the rest of the way to Lake Rosalie. Our first trip had broken loose all the hyacinth jams, and the current had washed them all out. The creek was practically clear. The game wardens told us we were the first ones to traverse the creek in more than twenty years.

We soon simplified our routine so that we'd take the boat to Walk-in-Water Lake, where I'd run the hooks while Buddy drove the van to Lake Rosalie to wait for me. We'd skin the day's catch of gators and be home before dark. We were catching eight or ten gators every day. They would run from six to twelve feet long. If the bait was down, I would catch the rope and gently raise the gator's head to the surface. The trick was to shoot it in the head before it had a chance to realize what was happening.

A ten-foot gator is about twice as heavy as a nine-footer, and a twelve-foot gator is about four times the size of a ten-footer. I loaded gators into the boat up to ten feet long, but the larger ones I had to skin on the spot.

Gator hides were bringing two dollars a foot at that time, but only one dollar if they had buttons. We were making more than a hundred dollars a day—not bad considering the best wage we could expect at that time was thirty-five dollars a week.

My wife, June, had never seen a gator caught on a hook, and I took her with me one time. The first hook we came to was down, but the rope was still coiled up at the foot of the tree it was tied to. I could tell the gator had just taken the bait and didn't know it was hooked yet.

Ordinarily I would have slipped in, given the rope a good jerk to startle the gator, and got back out of the way until it had worn itself out before attempting to take it. But I thought June might enjoy seeing how a freshly caught gator acts, so I told her to catch the rope and pull the gator's head up so I could shoot it. I also told her, regardless of what happened, to stay seated in the bow—that if she tried to move around she might turn the boat over.

She grabbed the rope, gave it a good tug, and started bringing it in hand over hand. I could see the slack was coming in the rope a lot faster than she was bringing it in, and I had a good idea what was fixing to happen, so I eased the motor into reverse and got ready to open the throttle to get out of the gator's way. I didn't get in too big a hurry, because I didn't want to deprive June of a close look.

A twelve-foot gator that weighed about four hundred pounds exploded out of the water about six inches from June's face. It came up about six feet above the water, hit the side of the boat with a terrible jolt, and just missed coming completely into the boat. June squealed one time, and the next thing I knew she was draped all over me so I couldn't even see the gator, which was running and jumping like a blue marlin and tearing up the shoreline. I tried not to let her see me laughing, but it was a sight I will never forget, and I'm sure June won't either.

On one trip, as I was running the hooks I came across a gator that hadn't swallowed the bait but had hooked itself in the foot. I'd heard they were paying good money for live gators at a gator farm in St. Augustine, so I decided to bring it in alive.

You can hold a gator's mouth shut easily with two fingers, but nothing in the world can hold it open. I've seen them when we got them in the close circle of a net swimming around crunching every hard-shell turtle they bumped into like it was an eggshell. If you can get its mouth tied shut, the gator will lie quietly most anywhere you put it, and you can handle it easily.

I eased the head up to the side of the boat and slipped a nylon cord noose over the bill. The gator tried to open its mouth two or three times, then just sort of relaxed. I worked the hook out of its foot and slid the gator over into the boat and laid it down amongst the other gators, with a dead gator on each side. It was nine feet long.

I finished running the hooks and pulled up to the shore where Buddy was waiting. I told him to start dragging them out so we could start skinning. I pretended to be fixing the motor because I wanted to see his reaction when he came across the live gator. I always covered the gators with cabbage palm leaves to keep the sun from burning them. There were six or seven dead gators along with the live one. We always laid them out in the boat with the heads toward the bow.

Buddy reached up under the cabbage fans, grabbed a gator by the bill, slid it out on the ground, and reached for another one.

He grabbed the live gator!

The gator raised up on all four feet, stuck its head up through the cabbage fans, and snorted like a scared buck. Buddy set a new world record for the hundred-yard dash getting to the woods, and it took me about twenty minutes to coax him back to the boat. I had to load the live gator in the van before he'd come back. He was shaking so hard I had to skin all the gators by myself. He was paralyzed! When we got through skinning, and were ready to take the live gator to St. Augustine, Buddy made me tie a piece of plywood up to separate the cargo area from the seats before he'd get in the van.

June and I lived directly across the street from Jimmy's Bar, in an apartment upstairs over Lawyer Thacker's office. There was a balcony out front

a

where we'd sit and relax late in the afternoons. The only place to park the van that day was right in front of Jimmy's.

The gator had somehow knocked down the plywood divider, pushed the back of the driver's seat forward, and crawled up with its front feet on the steering wheel, and it was staring all around from side to side. It looked for all the world like it was sitting in the seat ready to drive.

Buddy, June, and I were watching, and just as the gator got into position, a drunk wandered out of Jimmy's, took one look, and whirled right around and went back inside. In just a minute about twenty people came pouring out of Jimmy's and gawked at the gator.

The gator just glared back at them and held on to the steering wheel!

 One summer Rossie and I were camping on Sand Beach on Lake Hatchineha. We were fishing baskets and trotlines and running gator hooks. There'd been a prolonged drought, and the water level was way down. We got to talking about all the gators that must be in Reedy Creek Swamp.

Reedy Creek emptied into Lake Hatchineha, but you couldn't get up it in a boat on account of it was choked up with water hyacinths. We didn't think that would be much of a problem because the swamp was dry and we could walk alongside the creek and look for gator holes. We got our gator rod ready, and at daylight the next morning we were at the mouth of Reedy.

A gator rod is a limber steel rod about twelve or fourteen feet long with a hook on one end. I had drilled a hole lengthwise through a two-foot length of hickory sapling and passed the other end of my rod through the hickory and welded a washer on the end. This way the rod could revolve freely while I was pulling on it by the hickory handle.

The way you catch a gator with a rod is to prod around in the gator hole until you make it mad, and it will start snapping at the rod. As soon as you feel the gator snap, you jerk the rod back and try to set the hook. They are not really all that hard to hook. As soon as you hook it, it will start twisting round and round, trying to get loose from the hook. It can twist real fast, so you have to be real careful not to get your clothes tangled up in the rod. We didn't wear many clothes anyway. If you maintain a steady pull on the rod, the gator will literally screw itself out of its hole and onto the ground, where you can shoot it with a .22 rifle.

We walked up into the swamp a couple of miles and came across a large gator hole. There were a lot of fresh signs, and this hole was teeming with fish and turtles. Rossie said, "LeRoy, this looks like a good one. Let's get him!"

The water level was about two feet down from the ground level, and I could just see the outline of the entrance to the gator's cave. We looked the situation over carefully and made our battle plan. The only way we could get to the mouth of the cave was to get down into the gator hole. I told Rossie to stay on the bank and I'd wade up to the mouth of the cave, hook the gator, hand the rod to him, extricate myself from the muddy gator hole, grab the rifle, and shoot the gator as soon as Rossie could get its head out of the water.

I took off my shirt to streamline me a little and crawled down into the gator hole. The water was deeper than I thought—a little past my waist. The bottom was spongy muck, and occasionally I'd sink up to my armpits. It was thirty or forty feet wide, but it looked like half a mile to me.

I inched my way gingerly up to the mouth of the cave. All kinds of critters were bumping into my legs and belly. Rossie was giving me instructions: Go this way, go that way a little. It wasn't bothering him a bit. I finally made it up to the mouth of the cave. He handed me the rod, and I began to probe around for the gator. It wasn't within reach of the rod.

There was a sort of brow that stuck out a few feet over the mouth of the cave. Rossie said he'd take the machete and cut off the brow so I could get in two or three feet closer and maybe reach the gator. He hacked on one side of the overhang a couple of times, then started on the other side. A piece about the size of three or four oil drums fell into the water and exposed a den of cottonmouth moccasins. There was more than a bushel basketful of them. It looked like every snake in Reedy Creek Swamp was gathered there. They were all twisted and knotted around each other.

As soon as the light hit them they started to disperse and fell into the water all around me. The water was covered with them, swimming around like crazy. It really gave me a thrill to look down about six inches from my face and see thirty or forty big moccasins crawling around my stomach.

I did my best to imitate a cypress stump. I didn't move a hair! The only movement I made was to raise goose bumps. I didn't even dare breathe for about thirty minutes until the snakes settled down a little. Rossie took a stick and carefully pushed the snakes aside to clear me a path to a place where I could crawl out.

I MADE IT!!

As soon as I got out reaction set in, and I started shaking like a leaf and got freezing cold. The temperature was about ninety degrees, but I was wet and made Rossie build a fire. He made some coffee, and after I had sipped a little and got warmed up, I started to recover and we began to form plan B. We knew it was a big gator by the size of the cave, and we wanted him real bad!

We went back to the cave, and I began to poke around about fifteen or twenty feet back from the mouth. I hit a spot where the roof was only six or eight inches thick. It must have been over the food shelf. I worked the rod down into the cave and poked around a little to determine how big the cave was.

The rod touched the gator's back. I knew instantly what I'd touched. Nothing else in the world feels like a rod sliding down a gator's back. I jerked the rod back to keep from disturbing the gator until we figured out how we were going to get it out.

I was too late! When I jerked the rod back, the gator bit the hook.

Rossie saw what I had done and rushed over to help me. We couldn't do a thing with the gator. It jerked us around any way it wanted to. We hung on for dear life. I did not want to lose my gator rod. It would pull us down until the handle was almost out of sight, and then we'd gain a little.

It started twisting in earnest then, and its head began to come through the roof of the cave. Rossie told me to let go, get the rifle, and shoot the gator. I grabbed the rifle, but my hands were so muddy and slick that I couldn't handle it properly. The rifle was an automatic, but there was a pin in the breech that, if pushed in, would only let it fire one shot. You had to work the breech by hand to fire again.

The first shot hit the heavy bone plate on top of its head, because the gator rolled just as I pulled the trigger. The bullet went *spang* as it ricocheted out through the cypress trees. The shot made the gator mad, and it tried harder to screw itself loose from the hook. Rossie kept hollering, "Shoot him again! Shoot him again!" I took dead aim and, just as the gator stopped for a second, pulled the trigger for a sure shot.

Nothing happened!

The pin in the breech had gotten pushed in during the struggle. My hands were so slippery I was having trouble operating the pin and the breech. The gator had its head and both front feet out of the top of the cave by now. It was truly a monster! Its head was more than three feet long.

Very shortly I managed to place a killing shot in its head. Rossie told me to throw the gun down and help him hold the gator—its dying twitches were threatening to pull him back into the cave. It finally quit twitching, and we stepped over to admire it.

The gator was lying there with just its head and front feet out of the ground. It measured about two and a half feet across the shoulders. We tried to pull it out, but we couldn't even budge it. Its head would have weighed three hundred pounds.

Rossie had a couple of gator hook ropes in the muzzle, a cloth sack also used to feed horses, that we carried our dinner and other incidentals in. They were three-eighths-inch grass ropes about twenty-five feet long. We tied one end around the neck and the other to a tree. We would swing on the rope and pull and try every way, but we still couldn't budge that gator.

We finally tied a rope around its neck with the loose end leading off to one side, passed the rope around a tree at about shoulder height, and tied it to the loop around the gator's neck on the opposite side.

We broke off a piece of cypress limb about four inches around and four feet long. We put the limb between the two ropes and started to twist them together. The gator began to slide out ever so gradually. As soon as we'd twisted the rope as far as we could, we'd untwist it, take up the slack, and repeat the operation. We performed this maneuver many times before we got

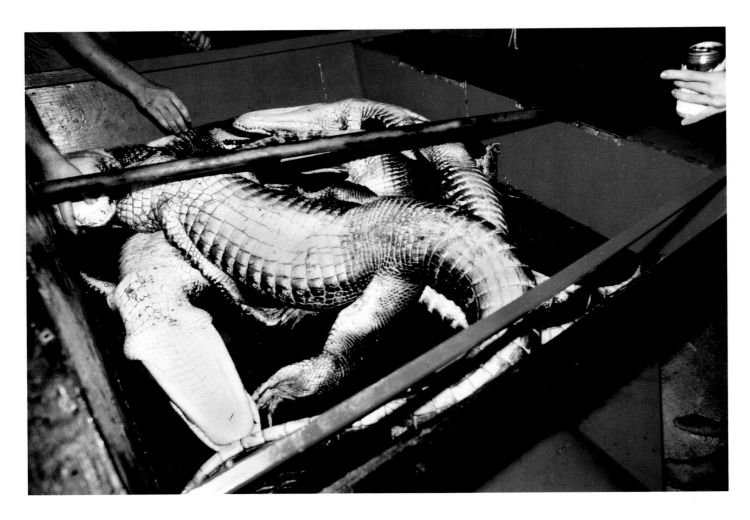

The Catch

All southern states control alligator hunting. Those with the denser alligator populations allow legal hunting on private lands in the spring and on public lands in the fall. The "catch" also means money for schoolbooks and supplies, vehicles, medical treatment, clothes, house repairs, leisure activities, and fishing boats or other hunting expenses. A minimal amount of alligator hunting is for trophies. Hunting is dangerous work and takes a water savvy that the average trophy hunter lacks without instruction and guidance from an experienced trapper.

the gator out. It was very fat—I estimated its weight at close to 1,200 pounds. The hide alone must've weighed around 100 pounds.

We had killed him about ten o'clock in the morning, and it was black dark by the time we got him skinned. We were at least two miles from the boat, and there's no dark any darker than Reedy Creek Swamp on a moonless night. I will never know how Rossie found the way to the boat. If it had been left up to me, we'd still be in there. I was too tired and confused to do any more than drag the hide my share of the way and stumble along behind Rossie.

The hide measured thirteen feet, ten inches. It had two buttons right in the middle of the belly. It sold for thirteen dollars!

A group of commercial fisherman would come by our camp about once every ten days or two weeks. We would join them and all go to Lake Kissimmee and fish a net. The Game and Fish Commission had closed the lake to net fishing but wasn't enforcing the law vigorously. We would seine at night to lessen the danger of some sport fishermen reporting us.

Quite often we would catch alligators in the net. They usually weren't much of a problem. We would hold the cork line down underwater, and the gator would swim out. One moonlit night as we pulled the net in a close circle, we noticed a large gator swimming around among the fish and turtles. It was not acting as docile as gators ordinarily do. It would bump into a turtle and, instead of turning or ignoring it, would crunch the turtle up. It was circling around as the net circle grew smaller and smaller. It had us all trying every way we could think of to get it out; it would come up to the cork line, but when we held it down for it to swim out, it would turn around and go back. Shoals of fish would escape everytime we tried to get the gator out.

Rossie said, "Y'all try to drive him over to me. We're going to lose all the fish if we don't get him out pretty quick!" When the gator came by Rossie reached out with one hand, caught the gator by the bill, and pulled it over the cork line. The gator just swam off.

The next day Rossie told me the gator tried several times to open its mouth but didn't even try to do anything else. It seemed that since it couldn't get its mouth open, it forgot about its powerful tail and legs. It was about nine or ten feet long and probably weighed 250 pounds.

Rossie practiced on every gator we caught after that, locating the exact spot on the neck where he could stick a pocketknife to penetrate the spinal cord and kill the gator. The next time we got a gator in the net Tom Thornton said, "All right Rossie, show us how to do it." Rossie reached over in the net, grabbed the gator by the bill with his left hand, and stuck the knife in with his right hand. The gator died instantly, just like it had been shot.

None of the rest of us had the guts to try this stunt. I practiced on dead gators a lot, but I could never make myself try on a live one. Rossie was

assured a place on the net crew from then on. No one would go fishing any-more unless he was along.

Frog legs were bringing a dollar a pound, and some of the easiest money we could make was frog hunting. Frogs and gators inhabit the same areas in a marsh. We hated to have to pass up all the gators just because we couldn't use a gun at night anymore.

I built a harpoon that was tied to the small end of a push pole with a piece of twine. The harpoon was tied to a five-gallon oil can by a twenty-five-foot piece of rope. I'd pole up to the gator, stick the harpoon in it, and pull on the push pole to break the string and release the harpoon. Then I'd throw the can overboard and come back in the morning to retrieve the gator. I'd try to place the harpoon into the rib cage from the shoulder. The gator would die very quickly.

Eddie Seaver and I were operating a sport fishing camp at Blue Cypress Lake in 1956 when we heard that the Game and Fish Commission was going to stop all gator harvesting in Florida. Some biologist had declared that alligators were almost extinct. He reported there were so few of them left that they should be put on the endangered species list. He predicted it would take fifty years for the gators to repopulate Florida to the point where they could be taken off the list. I don't know where he got his information. He certainly wasn't aware of the gator population of Reedy Creek Swamp and hundreds more similar swamps.

I went into Reedy Creek Swamp once to try to figure out some way to operate a gator hunting expedition in there. I went into the swamp near Loughman and traveled in an easterly direction for two days until I found some high ground to sleep on. The next morning I started making a big circle to the south on my way back out.

Before dark on the third night, I came to a large area that had a gator hole about every fifty yards. There were literally hundreds. Every direction I went in, I found gator holes, on and on. The water table was low, but not nearly as low as in a drought. I had been in water from ankle deep to over my head for three days.

Looking at all those gator holes made my mouth water to hunt them, but I could not figure any way to get them out. I found a big cypress log that had fallen down. It was about fifteen feet in diameter. I climbed up on top of it, built a fire, and cooked a fox squirrel for supper. I had one sweet potato and one biscuit left. I ate the sweet potato and most of the squirrel and saved the biscuit for breakfast. I could see five large gator holes from where I was sitting on top of the log.

The next morning, I counted more than a hundred gators lying around everywhere, ranging in size from two feet to monsters. There was no danger

The Weigh-in

Traditional alligator hunting engages members of the family and of the community. Youngsters learn by watching their parents, relatives, and friends and by taking part as their neighbors work together to reap the annual harvest. When check stations operated during the experimental hunts—1981 to 1990—from dusk until late in the night while the hunters were on the water, often past midnight, the community gathered at the boat ramps anticipating their return. There a mix of hunter families, curious onlookers, wildlife officers, researchers, and members of the press all socialized and interacted. When the hunters arrived the weigh-in was an exciting event characterized by celebration and by curiosity about the catch. In years past they off-loaded their catch onto huge scales for weighing and measuring. Current practice is to compute the total body weight based on the processed meat. Each alligator must be assigned a numbered tag for tracking through the skin auction and meat sale. Although the check stations are no longer used, when the hunters return the atmosphere is charged with energy and physicality as heavy animals are moved from the boats to trucks for transport to coolers until they are moved to the processing houses, where skinning and butchering begin.

of these gators ever becoming extinct—there simply wasn't any way to get them out.

I decided to give up my quest and make a beeline for where I thought the truck was. When I got about a mile from the edge of the swamp, I heard people hollering and cracking whips, and I couldn't figure out what was going on. I hurried as fast as I could go and got out of the swamp in about half an hour. It was about one o'clock. Some friends had found my truck the day before, and since I hadn't come out yet, they'd organized a search party to come hunt for me. After that I tried to remember to tell someone if I planned to stay in the swamps overnight. I had seen evidence of enough gators in that one swamp to repopulate Florida and a few other states. The year was 1953.

It was winter and our camp, built on piers out over the water, had a large screened-in porch on the south side. We had let the canvas covers down over the screens and got a good fire going in the wood stove. We started discussing the closing of gator hunting. The season was to open June first and close January first. It would be the last season ever for gator hunting. We decided we'd get all our affairs in order so we could spend the summer hunting gators.

We got a late start on June first. We went to a small lake in Polk County, about eight or ten miles out from Haines City toward Polk City. We set hooks all around and decided to call it a day.

The next morning early we set out to run the hooks and then split up to set hooks in the other lakes. Eddie would take his boat and start around a lake, I would go around the other side, and when we met we would come straight across the lake, load up, and move on to another lake. We figured that since this was to be the last gator hunt, we would give it our very best shot.

We left my boat at the landing and launched Eddie's. After we had gotten under way we discovered that Eddie had left his good rifle at home and the only rifle in the boat was an old relic of a single-shot. The only cartridges were part of a box we found floating around in the bottom of the boat.

You have to run gator hooks every day, because sometimes a gator will lunge trying to get loose after it swallows the bait. The hook will tear up through the heart and lungs, and it will die quickly. The sun will burn the hide and make it unfit for sale.

Around on the south side of the lake was a steep muck bank where the water was about four feet below a sheer drop-off from the bank. We could run the boat right up to the bank. We had set a hook there.

As we approached the bank we could see a very large gator lying out on the bank. Eddie said, "Looka yonda, what a gator! He's crawled out on the bank and died!" I said, "Eddie, I'm not so sure about that. Hold up a minute and I'll put a bullet in his head to make sure." Eddie replied, "Oh, he's dead, grab that limb sticking out over the water there," as he pulled the boat up parallel to the bank and prepared to get out.

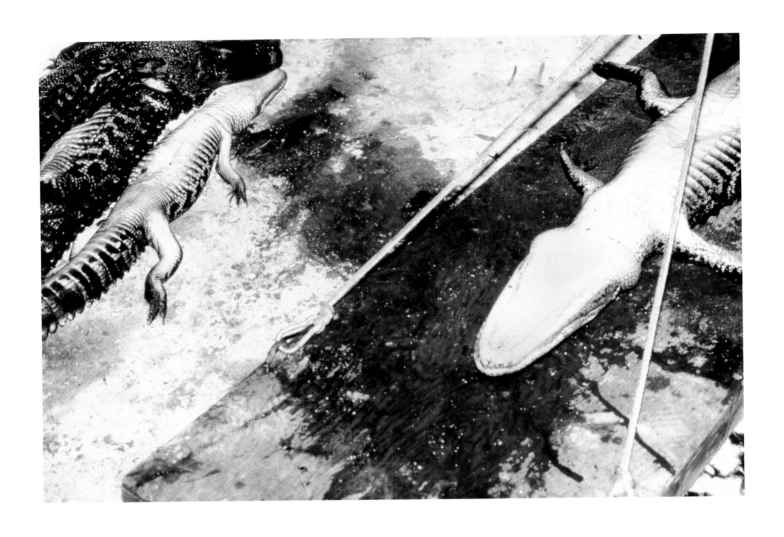

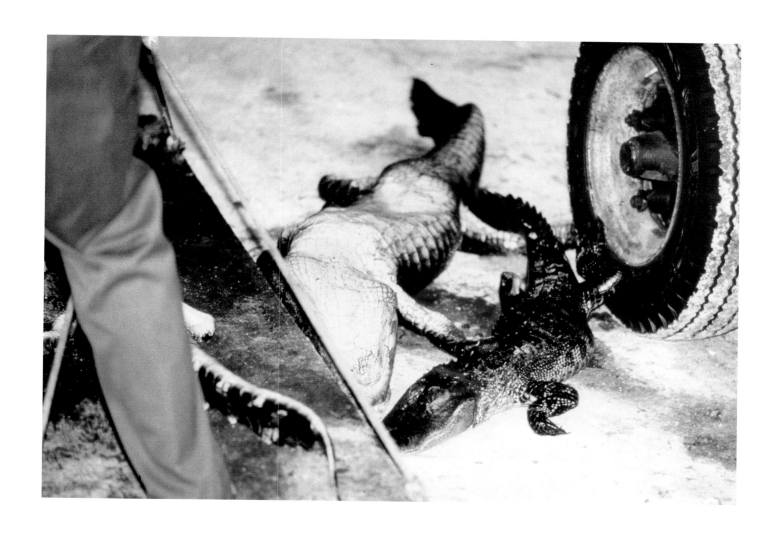

The gator came to life and roared off the bank like a freight train, into the boat and over the other side into the lake, right between Eddie and me. The rope broke like twine when the gator got to the end of it. The boat was over half full of water and about to sink, the oars and a can of bait were floating in the lake, and the rifle and shells were in the bottom of the boat underwater. We grabbed a bucket apiece and soon had the boat bailed out and most of our equipment rounded up.

There was no wind that day, and we noticed a line of bubbles leading off the way the gator had gone. About that time the gator surfaced for air, and Eddie said, "Shoot him! Shoot him!" I had been trying to get the rifle back in working order, and I raised it up and pulled the trigger. When the gun went off it sounded like a toy cap pistol—a little water shot out of the barrel, and I could have stopped the bullet with my bare hand. The gator dived back down, and Eddie grabbed an oar, jumped up in the bow, and started following the bubble trail.

Ordinarily a gator can stay underwater for more than an hour. The hook had apparently damaged its lungs pretty badly, because in a few minutes it surfaced again. It was only about ten feet ahead of the boat. The gun misfired! We tried about five more times before I finally got a bullet to fire properly and killed it. Eddie had stayed on the bubble trail all that time, and when the gator surfaced we were always ten to twenty feet away from it.

The bubbles were coming up from the bottom in one spot now, and we used a drag hook for a weight tied by a long string to an oar for a float to mark the spot. We crossed the lake to where there was a tall stand of bay trees. We cut a bay sapling about fourteen feet long and nailed a gator hook to the end of it. Then we went back, located the gator, and fished him up. The water was about ten feet deep, and it took all both of us could do just to raise it to the surface.

We finally got the bay sapling bent over the side of the boat, and Eddie held it while I got in the water and tied a rope around the gator's neck and then to the stern of the boat. Eddie worked the hook out and we towed the gator to the landing. We tied a tow chain around its neck, hooked it to the van, and dragged the gator out under a big live oak tree.

We borrowed a box of .22 cartridges from the resident fisherman and went back to run the rest of our hooks. We caught three more gators the same size as the first one. Everything went by the book, and we didn't have any more trouble. We would catch a gator, tow it to the launching ramp, drag it out under the live oak, and return to the hook line.

As we towed the last gator in, we noticed that a crowd had gathered at the landing. One man told me a man had come by his place and told him that two fellas were out at the lake bringing in twenty-foot gators as fast as they could go across the lake and come back. We measured the gators, and they were all fourteen feet or longer—all about the same size.

What I have been calling a van was actually a panel truck. It had doors across the back that opened up to expose the whole cargo area, which measured about seven feet wide by twelve feet long.

We recruited about fifteen helpers from the crowd and managed to slide the gators into the van. Two gators covered the whole floor, and we put the other two on top of them. The tails were hanging out the back about two feet, so Eddie got in and pulled the tails around, and I managed to get the doors shut. We decided to skin them at Ben Crawford's fish house, where he'd buy the hides afterward. Thus we'd have a chance to let our friends admire them.

The van was made to haul a big load, but I don't think Mr. GMC planned on its hauling four tons of gators. The tires were almost flat, and we had to pump them up to about sixty-five pounds pressure with the hand pump to make them stand up. It's a good thing we had Eddie's truck along too, because we had four flat tires before we got to Kissimmee.

We caught gators by the hundreds that summer. We'd move into a lake, set hooks all around, and as soon as our catch started dropping off, we'd move on to another lake. We caught just as many where there was a heavy population of people around the lake as we did in the undeveloped lakes.

We were setting hooks in a lake in Winter Haven when we caught a fourteen-footer. The hook was set about twenty yards from a dock, and on the other side of the dock was a swimming beach. The whole lake was ringed with swimming beaches. The woman who owned the lot came down to talk to us as we were tying on to the gator to drag it to a place where we could skin it. She said, "My God! Do you mean I've been going swimming every day with a monster like that? I won't ever get in the water again!" We caught about twenty others there before we moved on, and there were plenty left.

I've wished many times that we had taken some photographs of the gators we caught that summer. It was the last gator hunt ever for us. I would give a lot for just one picture of the four fourteen-footers we took to Ben's fish house to skin. I had no idea at the time that this would be one of the greatest adventures of my life and that I would recall the memory of it with such nostalgia. Later in life when I took up marlin fishing seriously, I had pictures made of everything. I flip through my scrapbooks regularly, and pictures make the memories so much more enjoyable.

I predicted that within twenty years of the closing of the alligator harvest the gators would multiply to such numbers that they would be a nuisance and a danger to the public. I still can't understand how the biologists could be so wrong or where they acquired the information they used to justify the decision that was made.

LeRoy Overstreet

Memories
of Gator Hunts

One large female will lay, on average, thirty to forty or fifty eggs every year—sometimes she will lay as many as sixty. Most if not all will hatch unless preyed on by raccoons. The female protects her eggs and young religiously until they are old enough to fend for themselves. I believe she would attack a battleship if it threatened her young.

Nowadays we hear about a gator attacking a swimmer every so often. I strongly suspect that the person inadvertently swims into the space a mama gator feels she must guard to protect her young. Poodles, retrievers, and other dogs, on the other hand, must simply look like good eatin'.

At the time Eddie and I were running the fish camp at Blue Cypress, there was another fish camp about two hundred yards south of us. The man who ran it had the first name Don. I can't recall his last name.

Don was in a canal that led off from the lake when he saw several small gators. He thought he would catch a couple to take home so his little daughter could play with them. He reached down in the water and grabbed a gator. It grunted three or four times like they do to call their mama. The mama charged out from her hiding place like a mountain lion and attacked the boat. She bit a big piece out of the bow and broke some of the main frame structures. If Don had not been in a skipjack she would have sunk him on the spot. She continued to attack the boat, while Don kept pushing at her with his pole, until he threw the little gator back. Don decided his daughter didn't need a young gator for a pet.

The only other time a gator will attack a person is if someone feeds it. The gator starts associating food with people. It gets so every time the gator sees a person it expects to be fed. It can't tell the one who feeds it from any other person. It just expects to get fed, and if you don't feed it the gator will eat you.

Hunters and trappers will tell you there were no problem gators until people started feeding them marshmallows and the like. They will tell you that, in the wild, gators are afraid of people. Once people start to feed them, they lose this fear quickly, and the hand that feeds them is just another meal. Gators are not intelligent enough to know the difference.

The last unprovoked gator attack in Alabama was to a man in Conecuh National Forest at a public land-use area in Covington County. He was hot, so he went into a pond and was splashing around to cool off when a large gator attacked and twisted off his arm.

Ordinarily, a wild gator would get far away from such actions as fast as he could. Could this gator have been conditioned to expect a few fish heads thrown to him by some well-meaning fisherman? Or some picnic scraps tossed by some campers? Could the splash in the water have triggered the gator's expectation that food would appear?

It is going to be interesting to see how the powers that be cope with the coming gator population explosion. People are moving into gators' territories, building houses on the lakeshores where they used to mate and bellow.

We are destroying the gators' food source of rabbits, raccoons, opossums, and other critters. We are clearing the grass along the lakeshores where the gators used to lie in wait for the critters to walk out on the log to get a drink and are turning them into swimming beaches.

Since I am seventy years old now, I know I will not be able to chase gators for many more years. I try to teach as much as I can to the younger generation, when I find someone who is interested, and to explain why I respectfully salute this most noble reptile, the alligator, one of the last living dinosaurs, whose supreme sacrifice provided so many of us with our livelihood during and after the Great Depression.

LeRoy Overstreet

Memories
of Gator Hunts

⚘ Products

Alligators are valuable for more than meat and leather goods. A diverse alligator industry services a variety of customers, and medical research and treatment create markets as well. A non-luxury benefit of alligator hunting is the ophthalmological research conducted using alligators' eyes, which physiologically resemble humans'. Researchers at the University of Florida, working on a molecular level, have been investigating the pigment in alligator eyes that catches light and creates nerve impulses. This pigment, rhodopsin, found in the rods, is

the same one that permits human night vision. By understanding how normal eyes function, researchers can learn how to fix impaired vision. The researchers work comparatively, mostly with cow eyes, but they use those of chickens, alligators, and amphibians as well. They have found that alligators' eyes are more like chickens' than like those of frogs and salamanders, for instance, an interesting sidelight on theories of alligators' descent.[18]

Jewelers use alligator bones, hide, claws, and teeth to create earrings, pins, necklaces, bracelets, bolos, hair bobs, and watchbands. Craft items like book-bindings, key rings, belt buckles, back scratchers, paperweights, and refrigerator magnets are made from hide, claws, whole feet, scutes, and bone. Even the heads generate income; taxidermy techniques can restore and preserve them. Mounted alligators are bought by science museums, wildlife centers, and restaurants for educational purposes and as curiosities. Gator heads and feet are sold as trophies and curios from the southern wetland and deepwater cultures where this dinosaurian descendant still lives, encouraging visitors to take home a reminder of the local lore.

Skins and meat compose the largest part of the alligator market. The raw product most sought historically is the "green hide"—not yet tanned, dyed, and finished. Exotic leather tanners experiment with many unusual products such as the skins normally discarded when fish are filleted, which have unique scale patterns, as do other exotic leathers like alligator, lizard, and snakeskin. Alligator hide is used to make accessories and apparel such as belts and hats, wallets, purses, eyeglass cases, boots and shoes, and inlays on vests and jackets.

Increasingly, alligator meat is used in restaurants and in the home, perhaps because of its novelty, but also because it is healthful, being high in protein and low in fat and sodium. The tasty meat is very mild, like veal with a seafood edge. It is most commonly prepared as fried morsels served with lemon or hot sauce. There are numerous other recipes, many developed in the past decade, as regional gourmets have taken delight in concocting new alligator dishes. Citrus-marinated ribs are grilled. Lengths of white tail meat are marinated, grilled, flambéed, and angle-sliced in exotic dishes with names like Fire in the Swamp (see page 167). Chunks of leg, backstrap, body, or neck meat are stewed and spiced Cajun style or cooked with wine, French style. Scallops cut from the tail or "tenderloin" are sautéed with shallots or garlic and served Italian style with pasta. Soups using alligator jowls with corn, okra, tomatoes, peppers, and other vegetables are spiced as gumbos or lightly flavored as nouvelle cuisine chowders. The possibilities are limited only by the imagination, and the number of cookbooks that include alligator recipes is growing.[19]

The alligator industry is relatively new as a regulated business. At the beginning of the twentieth century alligators were plentiful, but as hunters and trappers across the southern United States exploited them to earn their livelihoods, larger animals became so wary that their number appeared to decrease and hunting became more difficult. Alligator products, especially skins, became coveted. By 1967 the animals had diminished until alligators were placed on the endangered species list, yet they made an unprecedented rebound and were removed in different years throughout the South: Louisiana, 1975; Florida, 1977; Texas, 1984; the rest of the South, 1985. Since then ranches, farms, and seasonal and nuisance hunting have returned alligator products to the marketplace. At first the market looked lucrative, but according to the Florida Alligator Trappers Association and the American Alligator Cycle of Protection, overproduction during the late 1980s caused severe problems within the industry. The bottom fell out of the hide market in 1991, and in 1992 and 1993 meat sales were far ahead of skin sales, leaving a surplus of skins in storage until the hide market could return to a profitable level in 1994. In 1995 the market showed signs of stabilizing. In 1996, however, the market turned downward, once again making the meat from large gators worth more than the hides. Historically the hide market has been diverse, depending on the United States, Canada, and Europe, and current markets are having to be rebuilt within those traditional markets or expanded to include the Middle East and the Pacific Rim.[20]

The future is always uncertain, but cooperation between hide producers in the southern states is strengthening the industry, which is expected to continue to improve as the market is cultivated. Unlike the situation earlier in the century, however, alligators are being managed as a sustainable resource, so there are realistic expectations for their continuance as economic incentives develop.

Mating

Although alligators look dinosaurian, gnarled and tough, in their mating ritual they are strong, graceful, and supremely gentle. Courtship continues from late April through June, corresponding to climatic shifts, with the heaviest mating (copulation) activity occurring in May in most locations.

Out in a swamp during breeding season, eerie bellows roll across the wetlands as bull gators inflate their lungs, arch their tails, lift their snouts, and sound their mating calls. As their bodies vibrate, water drops dance across their backs, staccato in the sunlight.

Alligators are territorial; the males define their space and fight for breeding areas. Two males living in close proximity with females nearby creates an inevitable fight for dominance. Once territory is established, mating begins: A sequence of gentle nudging and nuzzling ensues as the male and female float up and down in the water together in graceful slow motion.

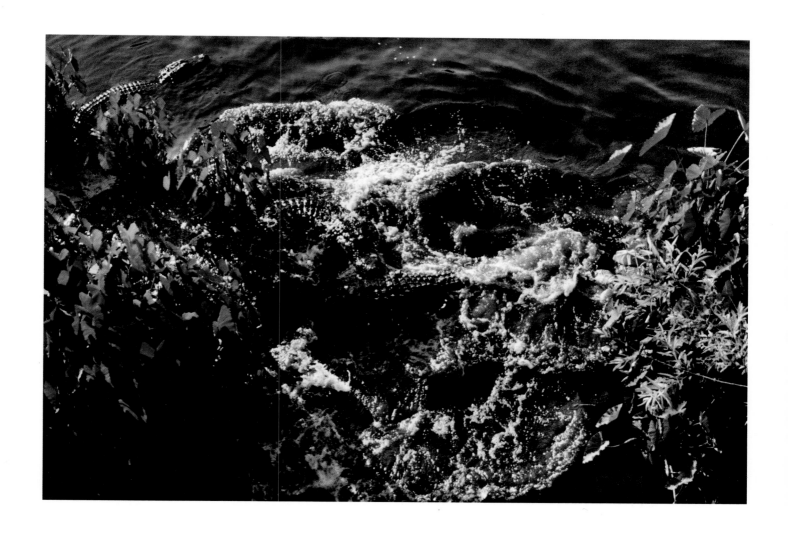

Baby Gators

Newly hatched alligators are only about nine to ten inches long, but they already have tiny needlelike teeth. They are not a solid color; instead their bodies are camouflaged with yellow-and-black markings that fade as they get older. Blending in with the sunlit grasses and reeds that grow out of the blackwaters, baby gators can be heard before they are seen.

Immediately after coming out of the nest, they head for the water and instinctively feed on crayfish, snails, fish, tadpoles, water bugs, spiders, and other small prey. For the first year they stay within close range of their mother. Although she does not feed them, she responds to their cries and protects them for several months. As they crawl over lily pads, scurry through the muck, and swim between the reeds, they make a chirp-grunt. In grown alligators this is usually a distress cry, but in babies, unless the intensity increases, their mother shows no interest. When traveling the aquatic regions of the southern states in a canoe or kayak, you occasionally can hear those cries and, just as the mother does, you can find the nesting area. Keep an eye out though, because where the baby gators are, so is the protective mother.

Alligators' characteristics concerning territorial selection, mating, maternal protection, number of eggs produced, and percentage of juveniles that survive have all contributed to the regeneration of the alligator population. Thirty years ago the American alligator was thought by many biologists and conservationists to be endangered or threatened and was protected by federal and state laws. Its subsequent increase was unexpected to many scientists and hunters alike. Factors contributing to its fast comeback are its prolific egg production; the attentive attitude of mother gators; its loud mating bellows, allowing the males and females

to find each other during breeding season; and the animals' travel patterns. At two years of age young alligators spend a year or so wandering around before they settle in an area that becomes their territory. As their numbers in an area increase and the alligators redistribute themselves in suitable population density, they create gator trails. Throughout the southern wetlands those who are observant may see trails that are used regularly as alligators travel within their territorial ranges.

⚙ Resource Management

Early traders in Florida, such as William Henry Brown and Jane Brown, who established Brown's Boat Landing in 1901, lived amid the indigenous grassy waters. Today the site of Brown's Boat Landing is on dry land, along a state highway running through the Big Cypress Seminole Indian Reservation pasturelands that were drained to raise cattle. Looking down on the "boat landing" from the air, you see pasturelands rimmed by orange groves and sugarcane fields. Vistas are etched by silver ribbons—the canals— that form the drainage system designed and built over the past hundred years.

Originally the landing was on an acre of high ground that the Browns cleared for a house, store, barn, and outbuildings. The store was made accessible to the deep water some hundred yards beyond by way of a shallow canal, dug so that the Seminoles could pole their dugouts right up to the front steps of the store. Brown's Boat Landing store, at the head of canoe navigation on the western edge of the glades, was complemented by Shorter's store and landing on the southwestern corner of the Everglades, Raulerson's store on Taylor Creek in the vicinity of the present town of Okeechobee, Stranahan's store in Fort Lauderdale, and Brickell's and

Girtman's stores in Miami. Though these were not the only stores in Miami, they were the centers of Seminole trading activity there before and after the turn of the twentieth century, respectively. Because a canoe trip from one side of the glades to the other meant four days' travel in each direction, having stores strategically positioned at the four corners of the area provided healthy markets for each and made marketing trips shorter for the Seminoles.[21]

The goods Seminoles commonly traded at the stores included alligator hides and teeth; pelts from deer, otters, raccoons, and occasionally skunks; plumes from snowy egrets, roseate spoonbills, and green and gold parakeets; diamond terrapins; sweet potatoes, pumpkins, and kunti.[22] Lemon seeds from the hammock groves were resold to nurseries for growing grafting stock for other citrus trees. Grasshoppers, wasps, bees, and beetles were also traded and shipped, packed in formaldehyde, to the American Entomological Company in Brooklyn, New York.[23]

The Lacey Act of 1900 placed plumed birds under protection, but in the far reaches of the swamps traversed by canoes, in a time when the fashion market paid high prices, the law simply drove prices up by creating an illicit market.[24] It was up to the traders to refuse to buy or trade for the plumes: some did just that, others did not.

Alligator skins came under early resource management by W. H. Brown's conservation economics. The policy at the Boat Landing was to encourage taking only five- to eight-foot gators; Brown paid fifty cents apiece for five-foot gators, seventy-five cents for six-foot gators, and ninety cents for those eight

feet and longer. Kersey writes, "This worked as sort of an economic check on overkilling the smaller breeding gators; also, there is no report that Brown ever bought baby gators for the tourist trade."[25] Although Brown's intent was admirable, because he lacked the information we currently have, his practice actually worked against a strong sustainable population. In fact, baby gators are the most expendable. The five- to nine-foot gators are the most valuable to the population.

In the glades, however, alligators were slaughtered by the thousands. Without laws to protect them, within fifty years they were hunted to alarmingly lower numbers. The story goes that during a drought when the wetlands had dried up, concentrating the alligators in deepwater lakes and gator holes, a group of Seminoles borrowed the Browns' oxcarts. On a four-week journey from the Boat Landing to Shorter's store in the south glades and back again, they killed 1,400 alligators, trading approximately 700 hides at each store.

When Congress approved on 28 September 1850 what is generally referred to as the Swamp and Overflowed Lands Grant Act, the intent was to improve large areas of land owned by the federal government. The purpose of granting these lands to the states was to encourage their reclamation through construction of levees and drains, which would be paid for by sale to private parties.[26]

In Florida this meant twenty million acres, including the Everglades. The earlier bill proposed by J. D. Wescott had pertained only to Florida's wetlands, but the 1850 act achieved the same result and applied to other states as well. Wescott believed like others that draining the state's wetlands would ensure the growth of a new agricultural empire in south Florida.

These early development efforts were conceived and executed by persons lacking the knowledge currently available regarding consequences to the environment. Though they were uninformed, their interests were to create the most fertile and productive lands within the United States. Even now, however, in the context of much ecological information, corporate agriculture, land development, and other business and private concerns continue to wreak havoc on our environment, demonstrating little understanding of or responsibility for the serious damage they cause.

CONSERVATION PLEDGE

I give my
Pledge as an American
To Save and Faithfully to
Defend from Waste the
Natural Resources of
My Country—Its Soil
and Minerals. Its
Forests. Waters.
and Wildlife.[27]

I think that good people have reacted to historical economic and social circumstances with laudable intentions to make a better world for themselves and their children. Some of these people have had a wider vision and an innate sense of what would sustain our natural resources. Some have been less visionary. Some are just so hungry for more wealth that they remain ignorant and fail to see the harm they cause.

As our country has developed, American imagination and industriousness have both benefited and damaged the quality of our lives. Each of us plays a role: we enjoy the amenities and advantages that various forms of progress have brought us. Science has also helped us understand how we have hurt our environment and ourselves. Observant naturalists and researchers who have spent time in the field have recognized the damage we have done, and they have proposed reasonable and effective measures to correct our mistakes. Many people have missed these experiences or lack the knowledge to grasp the complete picture. For example, some see only a threat to immediate economic advantages; they do not comprehend the necessity of living in and with a landscape. Instead of reason, we have an outright fight for and against nature, often with heightened emotions and exaggerated stances. Frequently information is manipulated to defend diverse positions on the political spectrum. Complex issues are reduced to media "sound bites."

So here we are, about to enter the twenty-first century and a new millennium. We have volumes of reliable information. How can we stop the in-fighting and look forward to providing for all species in a sustainable healthy environment? How can we create a win-win relationship between economics and environmental health? This must be possible. There must be an awakening whereby we sustain both our democracy and our native lands. We have the information, and we have people with the skills and the wisdom to guide us. We have communications systems that can make information accessible to millions: some television programming already addresses this goal. We are in a good position to become better informed and wiser about how we choose our future.

Conservation of natural resources is working for some wildlife species that people value highly, such as the bald eagle, peregrine falcon, grey wolf, brown pelican, and American alligator. Alligators have increased and the population has stabilized in most southern states, even as more land is drained for cattle, sugarcane, citrus groves, and residential and business communities. Many longtime residents of the wetlands want a larger alligator industry. The Louisiana Department of Wildlife and Fisheries, for example, has been a pioneer agency in research toward development of such an

industry, with Florida's Game and Fresh Water Fish Commission close behind.

Mike Fagan, president of the American Alligator Cycle of Protection, with years of experience as a nuisance control alligator hunter in central Florida, suggests changing the way drainage ditches are structured and maintained. Referring to the thousands of miles of such ditches in Florida, he proposes that if their banks were slanted instead of dug straight down, then saw grass, cattails, and other vegetation could grow on the sides and alligators could nest there. These plants would also support frogs, fish, turtles, and birds, all food for alligators, creating a sustainable habitat that would restore large areas of wetlands to Florida without loss of acreage for planting or grazing. The additional cost to landowners would be minimal and they could readily compensate by harvesting these new wetlands themselves or contracting out the harvest to others. Ideas similar to Fagan's have been put into use and are working. With the increase in alligators, the next item on our conservation agenda is to learn to live more comfortably in the same environment with them—to design and plan with nature at the same time as we make a living.

⫼ Effects of Human Population

As participants in the ecosystem, both alligators and humans claim territory in the aquatic habitat. Alligators select territory based on ecological appropriateness; people may select territory similarly, but typically they consider economics, status, and pleasure rather than ecology.

In Florida the Seminole Big Cypress Hunting Adventure lands harbor few alligators and provide none for hunting, because that section of the wetlands is now dry pasture and farmland. Large areas of the Everglades are drained by an extensive canal system that has been in place since the 1930s. Massive reservoirs by law are now being developed on new agricultural lands to clean waters that are fertilizer-rich and polluted with pesticides. The goal is to reduce the concentration of pollutants before the water flows into the many lakes and streams that are such a major asset to Florida's overall beauty. The economic prosperity of cattle ranches, citrus groves, and sugarcane farms results directly from the drainage of millions of acres in Florida. Similar dilemmas exist in other southern states.

People need places to live, work, and play, and wetlands are prime locations for developers eager to build new communities. But where is the education informing us that we are in the alligators' habitat, where swimming can be dangerous because we are invading their haunts? What dispersement of information about living with alligators is effective? Lakes and rivers with high density of alligators are dangerous, and people need to be aware of this. What will make people realize how important it is never to feed an alligator? Historically, people living in the southern wetlands possessed practical knowledge about coexisting with the wildlife native to their shared habitat. As people migrate into new areas, their wild neighbors change. A new environment and new neighbors mean people must learn new habits of coexistence or the biotic cycle will break down.

Currently, when people believe their pets or children are threatened by a gator, the nuisance trapper is called in to kill it or, less likely, remove it. When a pool is built in a wetlands area, where is the enforcement of a fence law so the gator will not end up in the pool? When tourism and industries are developed along the coast, who makes and enforces laws to reduce pollution of the nearby waterways? As communities develop, where is effective public education that helps people adjust their lifestyles to accommodate the needs of their wild neighbors? If such questions could be answered effectively, then people, alligators, and other wetland species could coexist. Land could be managed to benefit all living organisms. Understanding such basic interrelations with our biotic community could foster personal desire to act on a collective land ethic. Then all species could prosper.

Seasoned trappers and scientists will tell you that feeding alligators is dangerous because it speeds their getting used to being around people. Alligators are not pets; they cannot be tamed. They are neither smart nor inherently mean. In their massive bodies their brains are about the size of a walnut, and their behavior is governed by instinct. Alligators that get used to being around people lose their wild response to remain distant. Through habit they can become trained to be less wary of humans. Alligators can also become conditioned to expect food in a particular place, and they will eat any smaller animal that is available. If adults entertain themselves and their dog or child by feeding the alligator at the local pond, the pet or child may return alone, looking like a food source to the alligator. Currently our practice is to punish the alligator rather than the (ir)responsible adult. Not feeding alligators protects them as well as pets and children.

Human livelihood is a central issue in habitat use. People enjoy the same aquatic environments that are essential habitat for wetland and deepwater creatures. Water sports like swimming, fishing, and water skiing lure people to the sunny South, and part of the draw is the flora and fauna of the wetlands and the shorelines of the deepwater habitats. Real estate and agricultural development thus reaps billions of dollars annually with little or no concern for creating harmony or balance with the primeval, living landscape.

Housing developments in wetland locations could be a more positive part of the ecosystem if developers and homeowners would recognize the consequences of their actions and decisions and make constructive choices, supporting the health of all the animals and plants involved. A fence that separates a swimming pool from a wetland canal can protect people and pets from the wild animal and help prevent a nuisance capture. Coexistence is essential if we are to maintain the biotic cycle and sustain an ecological balance.

Water   *Gill Holland*

May the pattern of traditional rhythm be the order of the day like the serried tiles that lie in the seabottom of the pool. Vagaries will play across this alligator back like the swampy light that plays through this submerged orchard over which swimmers stroke. Frog said the trick in bringing a sleeping swamp gator off the sand up to the surface was to drift the canoe above into a parallel shadow, slip over the side, and lasso the snout and the tail with ropes that you then ease tight against the armor of the beast. Then very gently you hoist the sleeping log to the top where you have your woken, thrashing prisoner for the picnic and aquatic show and the concrete gator pool where Seminoles wrestle the beasts not selected for handbags or shoes. The tiles up and down the back of the alligator ran ripples in the light underwater like those tiles in the natatorium at the college where Laura took the pictures in a Jack Campbell waterproof throw-away camera that hangs on the wall over her canvas and on the other side of town over this typewriter, theoretically.[28]

Pollution

Alligators are physiologically responsive to chemical and environmental changes. Wetland and deepwater habitats, fertile and bountiful looking with an abundance of flora, may actually be filled with agricultural pollutants. Crystalline coastal waters wash ashore rubbish that can choke an animal.

Matagorda Island is one of the barrier islands along the Gulf of Mexico that protects the mainland from the great tides and strong waves of the open Gulf. It is separated from the mainland by San Antonio and Espíritu Santo bays. A wildlife management area and state park,

Matagorda is owned by federal and state governments and managed by the Texas Parks and Wildlife Department.

Nineteen species listed as threatened or endangered by state or federal governments are found on Matagorda Island, including whooping cranes, peregrine falcons, Ridley turtles, and horned lizards. The island is rich in wildlife such as fish and shellfish, birds, land and marine mammals (the most common being the bottle-nosed porpoise), and amphibians and reptiles (the largest being the American alligator).[29]

Matagorda's history is unique. Karankawa Indians used the island until the early half of the nineteenth century, when they were killed by disease or driven into Mexico by European settlers.[30] The Karankawa were described as often being six feet tall, carrying giant bows, and covered with dirt and alligator grease to repel mosquitoes, making them look fierce and imposing to Europeans such as Álvar Cabeza de Vaca, René-Robert Sieur de La Salle, and Jean Lafitte, all of whom visited the offshore island. Matagorda still retains vestiges of the past: remnants that played a part in the growth of Texas are the 1852 cast-iron lighthouse that

once served Indianola and Galveston, the now submerged Fort Esperanza, and the brick-lined canals called "military ditches" that zigzag across the island from the Gulf beach over the uplands to the bayside marshes, dating back to the Civil War.[31] These canals provide excellent environs for alligators, although they favor habitats scattered all over the island.

Industry, recreation, and tourism generate tons of trash every year. Much of that waste gets thrown overboard at sea and washes up on beaches, more obvious on shore than in the water. Used hypodermic needles, plastic wrappers, bottles, ropes, and chunks of Styrofoam are all negative and unnecessary remnants of human activity. This irresponsible trashing endangers the environment and its life-forms. Wildlife officers on Matagorda Island clean the beaches regularly. Along a two-mile stretch cleanups gather more than two tons of refuse each fall and each spring in an effort to maintain the beachfront.

All over the country cleanup efforts are aimed at improving our environment. The Center for Marine Conservation in Washington, D.C., has a Coastal Cleanup Division that helps coordinate and keep records on the coastal cleanups. Much of its concern is with solid waste, while other forms of waste are handled by the Environmental Protection Agency.[32]

Industrial, commercial, and agricultural pollution weakens the biotic system as sickness weakens the human body. Water and land become infected, and the biotic cycle becomes chemically and physically unbalanced. Such imbalances generate compensating reactions, throwing the whole cycle further off until the system's integrity is threatened, just as a person experiences a loss in the quality of life from repeated injury or illness.

An example is Lake Apopka in Florida. For nearly fifty years pesticides and agricultural wastes drained into the lake, slowly poisoning the water and weakening the biotic system. Then a chemical spill dealt a severe blow, further lowering the quality of the lake. Because the lake was damaged by both nutrient and toxic pollutants, restoration is extensive and slow. Nutrient pollutants make the lake overproductive, changing the floral and faunal structure of its life-forms. This generally reduces the diversity of species and favors those that can adapt to the changing nutrient levels. Toxic pollutants can kill species outright or affect their health over time, interfering with reproduction and survival. In the long term these two types of pollutants can alter the evolutionary process because of the domino effect throughout the biotic system of the lake. Regeneration will occur if habitat and natural cycles are restored and the flow of pesticides and toxic chemicals is significantly reduced. As the lake's quality improves, its life-forms can restore themselves and their natural cycles of regeneration and evolution.[33]

Fire and Fertility

In the concept of wilderness natural places may be said to be unspoiled or unaffected by human activity. Today, however, we know there is little if any area on the planet that is not affected by human beings on the ground and in the air. Usually we respond to obvious human alteration of the natural environment by terming the result artificial: hence the term "artificial nature" applies to a range of situations, from overt to more subtle changes in environments. Examples demonstrating this range are the created landscapes of zoos, the temperature- and humidity-controlled filtered environments

of heated and air-conditioned dwellings and vehicles, human-made lakes, football fields covered with Astroturf, and nature preserves. We refer to managed wildlife areas as nature preserves, projecting a perception of these areas as protected and unaffected wilderness, usually providing less restricted habitat for wild animals and more restricted habitat for humans.

The management of nature involves varying levels of control, and many examples are under scrutiny and in debate. Most stewards of such lands are influenced by scientists, politicians, private landowners, businesses, and the general populace, whose interests include preservation, conservation, politics, cultural integrity, recreation, and economics. Examples of habitat management are vegetation control methods such as regulating water levels and salinity and staging prescribed burns.

South Carolina and Louisiana have the biggest coastal impoundments of nature preserves in the Southeast. The principal management objective for these areas is to attract wintering waterfowl. Prescribed burns are meant to simulate the natural transformation of the ecosystem through fires started by lightning and spontaneous combustion. Present land management advocates three fire strategies—prevention, protection, and the use of fire for ecological benefits, in full partnership with other environmental factors—in order to have quality land management.[34]

The laws, policies, and regulations governing the southern wetlands and deepwater habitats and the wildlife therein have been major factors in the return and development of the American alligator, a natural treasure and a prominent feature of the landscape.

⫙⫙ Sustainable Use
of Natural Resources

Because European and American settlers
took the coastal lands of Florida and
drove the Seminoles inland into the Everglades, the indigenous Americans initially
began hunting and skinning alligators
to earn money to survive. Continued
unbridled hunting by Indians and others
nearly depleted the alligator resources.
Then the wetlands were drained for farming and cattle ranching, which adversely
affected alligator habitat.[35] Thus the
Seminole reservation lands provide little
suitable habitat to support a sustainable
commercial alligator harvest.

Jimmy McDaniel, a Creek Indian who
is a retired biologist for the state of
Florida, was hired by the Seminole Nation
as director of wildlife for all Seminole
lands. Recently McDaniel established a
private hunt business for the Seminoles,
called Big Cypress Hunting Adventures.
Game hunted on the Seminole Reservation lands includes white-tailed deer, Axis
stags, wild boars or piney woods rooters,
doves, snipes, and Osceola turkeys.

Hunting is a time-honored tradition in the lives and cultures of the Seminoles and other Indian nations. Another tradition is storytelling. Narrative history and instruction in various aspects of life use stories and legends. Hunting continues to be considered important in the lessons for several reasons. First, hunting is a past and present part of the lives of many "Amerindians." In some cases it is still a matter of survival. It is always a matter of survival for animals. While developing hunting skills, children learn about animals and are taught to be sensitive in their relations with them. Second, hunting exposes children to the differences between traditional Indian practices and the realities of modern hunting, and the important issues related to each. Third, because hunting is a continuing practice, a goal is to teach ways it can be managed to ensure that animal populations are maintained in a healthy state.[36]

One such legend coming out of the southeastern American Indian tradition is "The Alligator and the Hunter," also called "Alligator Power." This is a legend of the Choctaws, who lived in an area now part of the state of Mississippi.

This legend demonstrates the interrelation of species, the wisdom of sustainability, and respect for all life. The teaching imparts the knowledge that all living things on Earth are connected, no matter how different their lives are or how little they may seem to affect each other.

(An engraving by Theodore DeBry, based on a painting of Jacques le Moyne de Morgues, the artist who came to the New World with the Huguenots in 1564, depicts the drying of food by East Coast Indians, and illustrates the inclusion of alligator meat in the diet of indigenous Americans. See *The New World: The First Pictures of America,* by John White and Jacques le Moyne and engraved by Theodore DeBry, first published in London in 1591.)

The Alligator and the Hunter

Once there were many hunters living in a village, and most of them always brought home deer. But one hunter, though he often succeeded in getting close, had very bad luck, and the deer always escaped. On this particular hunting trip he had been away three days and had seen many deer, but he had not been able to kill a single one. He decided to go into the swamps, where there were many deer. When the sun was overhead on the fourth day, the hunter saw a large alligator resting on a dry, sandy spot.

The alligator's luck was even worse than his. The alligator had been without water for many days and was so weak it was almost dead. The man said, "My brother, what a terrible state you are in. I pity you." The alligator spoke in a voice that was very faint. "Is there any water nearby?" "Yes," replied the man. "In the forest, not far from here, is a deep pool of cool, clear spring water. There is always water there. If you go there you will always have water." "But I cannot travel there by myself. I am too weak. Come close so I can talk to you. You will come to no harm. Help me and I will help you," said the alligator.

The hunter went closer, although he was afraid of the alligator. Then the alligator spoke again. "I know you are a hunter who has been unable to kill any deer. If you carry me to the place of the water, I will teach you how to get a great many deer. You will be a great hunter. The hunter hesitated, then said, "My brother, I believe you will help me, but you are an alligator and I fear that you will scratch me or bite me. Let me bind your legs and jaws and then I will carry you." The alligator rolled over on its back and held up its legs, saying, "Do as you wish."

The hunter first bound the alligator's legs and then its jaws. Using great strength, he lifted the alligator to his shoulder and carried it to the deep, cool water where the springs never dried up. He placed the alligator on the ground near the water's edge, loosened the bindings, and stepped back. The alligator crawled into the water and dived underneath. The animal came up and dived back down three times, each time staying longer. At last it came to the surface and floated there, looking at the hunter who was seated on the bank.

"You have saved my life. I will help you, but you must do as I counsel. Then you will become a great hunter. Listen closely to me now. Take your bow and arrow into the woods. There you will meet a small doe. Do not kill it. It has not yet grown large enough to have young ones. Next, you will meet a large doe, but you must not kill this one either. You must again restrain your power as a hunter, because this doe has fawns who need care and will continue to have a young one every year. Then you will meet a small buck, but this one also must be spared. That buck will father many young ones. Greet it and continue on, and you will be an even greater hunter. At last you will meet a very large old buck that is ready to give itself to you. Kill that deer, and forever in the years to come, you will be able to kill many deer. You will be the greatest of hunters.

The hunter did as the alligator counseled. He went into the woods and met each deer, waiting until he met the large buck; then he killed it. Forever after, the hunter was the greatest hunter of them all, and he always had venison in his camp.

 **The Land**

Marsh   *Kevin Bezner*

The air is so heavy with it,
you can feel the ink,
the blue of the papermill's
ink. And yet
warblers skitter yellow
through palms, and great white
herons, pelicans, egrets fly low over
greening grasses.[37]

The Land as Habitat

Since the range of the American alligator encompasses the coastal states from Texas to North Carolina and occasionally extends into Oklahoma and Arkansas as well, the southern wetlands may be considered "alligator landscapes" in concept. These wetlands and deepwaters provide habitat for many creatures of the air, water, and land, including people. "Animal use" includes work, play, and procreation in an exquisite environment that is bountiful and beautiful. Responsible public and private landownership helps maintain a healthy habitat for wildlife. Alligators move throughout these territories in varying numbers, depending on the compatibility of the habitat. These alligator landscapes have diverse characteristics, demonstrating the adaptability of the American alligator, as the following descriptions reveal.

Part of the Big Cypress Seminole Indian Reservation in Florida, the Devil's Patio, is a unique limestone ground formation that resembles a poured concrete patio full of potholes. Named by biologist Jimmy McDaniel for its tricky surface, this formation was once a coral reef when south Florida was under the sea. The formation probably flattened once it was exposed to the weather over time. Though lush in vegetation and beautiful in structure, it is treacherous because the potholes are penetrated by dense tropical growth, making the surface difficult to see and traverse.

One of the oldest refuges in the National Wildlife Refuge system, St. Marks National Wildlife Refuge, established in 1931, lies along the Gulf of Mexico in northwest Florida, just south of Tallahassee. The refuge protects 65,000 acres of land and 32,000 acres of Apalachee Bay and includes diverse habitats. Salt marshes, tidal flats, and freshwater impoundments attract waterfowl and other water birds and are nurseries for fish, shrimp, and shellfish. Hardwood swamps provide nesting areas for wood ducks and night herons and homes for black bears, otters, and raccoons. Pine woods harbor turkeys, white-tailed deer, fox squirrels, and pine warblers. The marshes and swamps also support a large population of American alligators.[38]

In St. Marks Refuge history lives. Within its boundaries a lighthouse constructed in 1831 still operates, as does one of the oldest seine yards in Florida. West Goose Creek Seine Yard, 150 years old, is used for seining saltwater mullet. The remains of old evaporators and of the salt vats used by the Confederacy during the Civil War are also in St. Marks Refuge: salt was produced in Wakulla County by evaporating seawater. Highly significant are the Indian mounds scattered along the refuge coastline and up the Aucilla River, some dating back two thousand years. More recent human remains are found in Fort San Marcos de Apalachee, in the town of St. Marks where the Wakulla and St. Marks Rivers meet. The fort was built by the Spanish in 1679, then occupied by pirates and subsequently by British, Confederate, and federal forces during the following two hundred years.

In St. Marks Refuge, management techniques are applied to marsh and forest to create and enhance habitat for endan-

gered species, waterfowl, and other resident wildlife. An 18,000 acre section of tidal marsh, pinelands, and hardwood swamp was designated a wilderness area by Congress in 1975, however, and will always be protected for wildlife in its natural state.

Farther west along the Gulf Coast is the Little Chenier in southern Louisiana, east of State Highway 27. The land is owned by private and corporate interests and is heavily used for hunting and fishing. Much of Little Chenier is held as wetland and deepwater habitat, broken by ridge roads leading to the interior. Further access is only by boat. Whereas privately held land is generally "posted," corporation-owned land is open for public use as long as users obtain a permit from the corporation. Roadside fishing is allowed without a permit. The area is vast and beautiful. In summer blankets of flowers bloom profusely among the lush green water plants, stretching over miles of wetlands under skies dramatically filled with giant cloud formations. Warm, moist breezes carry the fragrance across lands where birds nest and people fish.

The name Myakka is derived from an Indian word meaning "big water." The Myakka River in Florida is a blackwater river whose amber stream begins at the Manatee-Hardee County line and widens as it flows sixty-three miles to empty into Charlotte Harbor between Venice and Fort Myers on the southwest coast of Florida. Myakka River State Park, established in 1942, is the largest state park in Florida, at present encompassing 28,875 acres. Twelve miles of the twisting, canopied river flow through the park, which abounds in native birds, deer, feral pigs, and alligators. Other fauna living along the river include the endangered wood stork, West Indian manatees, the threatened crested caracara, and species of special concern such as gopher tortoises and Florida gopher frogs.[39]

The Myakka River is extraordinarily scenic, distinguished by an in-stream sinkhole 150 feet deep at the base of Lower Myakka Lake. Little Salt Spring and Warm Mineral Springs have submerged caverns running into the river. The river's corridor includes the pine flatwoods mosaic of eastern Sarasota and Manatee Counties. Below the lakes, the river weaves through a hammock of oaks and cabbage palms. The hammock recedes, and brackish marsh rushes and grasses line the banks as the river approaches its tidal portion, twenty-three miles upstream from the mouth.

The Myakka is designated a state wild and scenic river; therefore it remains largely undeveloped. The river's banks may reveal a rich prehistoric record, since seventeen prehistoric sites have been informally identified and as yet remain unstudied. Also, the relative lack of development means most of its water is of good quality. The river is threatened by several concerns, though, such as possible phosphate mining in the headwaters, intensive agricultural runoff, urban runoff from existing development, and future development.

Because of the wild and scenic river designation the Myakka River Coordinating Council was created to study the river and develop a management plan to provide permanent protection and enhancement of the designated portion of the river. The state recognizes the Myakka River as a significant water system that needs special interagency coordination because wild and scenic rivers are becoming increasingly rare across the United States. Because it is a relatively pristine river close to an urban population, there is a great need to provide public education about the value of its qualities in order to retain them as this river, with its filigreed foliage and waters that mirror the dramatic beauty of the south Florida sky, draws increasing interest.[40]

Throughout Florida, in marshes and swamps and especially on shores near the coast, is that indomitable grass *Claudium jamaicensis*, saw grass. Saw grass is recognized by its coarse gray-green leaves, which are sawtoothed on the blade edges and midrib. The three-angled stems may grow three to ten feet and have flat, bladelike branches that are razor sharp as they whip around in the wind or as you move through them. The branches range from twelve to forty inches long and from a quarter inch to five-eighths of an inch wide. On top of the stems of mature plants, arrangements of flowers up to eight feet tall branch from an axis. The flowers mature into a round or oval, wrinkled nutlet about one-sixteenth of an inch long. This grass has stout runners, resulting in huge areas of grass extending as far as the eye can see. In the breeze these tall, densely growing shafts sway and rustle in unison, producing a sheet of sound that fluctuates with the wind currents.[41]

As alligators repeatedly crawl through this tall grass or across mucklands, they blaze "gator trails." Gator trails can easily be identified from the air, as you look down on the wetlands, or on the ground, when you find an opening in the grasses or a drag mark in the muck. Usually there will be a trail near a gator nest; or at the very least you might expect a gator in the vicinity. When you follow a gator trail into the saw grass on a lake, a machete helps, and so does a companion. The machete will reduce cuts and scratches on your body; the companion is for safety. In case one person falls through the vegetation mat into the gator's territory, if not its den, the second person can quickly help the swimmer get back on the floating land.

Alligator regeneration is significantly affected by climatic conditions. Temperature determines sex and population range. Excessive rain or drought threatens the viability of the habitat; in the rainy season of spring and early summer, water levels usually rise. In June and early July, female alligators build their nests by mounding vegetation. After laying typically thirty to fifty eggs, the female covers them with vegetation and muck for insulation. She stays nearby to protect her eggs from predators during the sixty-five days of incubation, then opens the nest and helps the babies to the water when they hatch.

The sex of alligators is determined by the temperature of the eggs during incubation, resulting in a pattern of female-male-female, with males produced at intermediate temperatures and females at low and high temperatures. The temperature range for incubation is 30°C/86°F to 34°C/93°F. The intermediate temperature for exclusive production of males is 32.5°C/90.5°F to 33°C/91.4°F. Smaller percentages of males are produced at temperatures as low as 31.5°C/88.7°F and

as high as 33.8°C/92.8°F. Between the two determining extremes, the ratio of females to males varies. The critical time for sex determination is thirty to forty-five days within the sixty-five days of incubation.[42]

Not all alligator nests are successful. Raccoons, opossums, snakes, skunks, otters, hogs, and bears may raid nests in spite of watchful mother alligators. In times of extended drought, nesting areas may dry up, or in periods of heavy rain they may flood. In severe droughts the water level can drop until the guard pool or den is exposed and dries up. This condition can also be perilous for a

mother gator guarding her nest, for when exposed to extreme heat, she may become heat stressed to the point of kicking the bucket if she doesn't leave.

When mother alligators hear the high-pitched chirp-grunts of the baby gators as they begin to hatch, they help free them by removing the nesting vegetation. The first two years of life are critical for the vulnerable small alligators, which can fall prey to larger animals including snakes, wading birds such as egrets, herons, ibises, and wood storks, raccoons, opossums, skunks, otters, large fish and bullfrogs, and even larger alligators.

Although threats to the survival of baby gators are numerous, they represent the alligator's function in the food chain. Baby gators furnish other wild animals in their wetland and deepwater habitats with the nourishment they need to live out their life cycles. Another alligator function is providing water in times of drought, further enriching the food chain population. When alligators dig in the mud during the dry season to find water, creating "gator holes," they frequently expose the only drinking water available for other animals. Over time, their continued digging and swishing around may turn these gator holes into small ponds that serve fish-eating birds, turtles, and other animals that drink and feed along with the alligator. Even farther down the food chain, small fish living in these larger gator holes feast on mosquito larvae produced when the rains return. Hence, by functioning on multiple subsistence levels, the alligator is a keystone creature in a wetland habitat, benefiting the wild order of nature.[43]

¡¡¡¡ Alligator Research

Alligators have been part of the biosphere for tens of thousands of years. Yet only in the past thirty-five years have the twenty-three species of crocodilians become more widely recognized as the fascinating and complex creatures they are. Scientists working internationally have combined efforts and shared information in all areas of research, including biology, chemistry, ecology, geography, economics, anthropology, and management. Of the two Alligatoridae, the American alligator (*Alligator mississippiensis*) is found only in the southern wetlands of the United States, and the Chinese alliga-

tor, Yangtze alligator, or tuo-long (*Alligator sinensis*) is found only in China. The Chinese alligator is an endangered species; the American alligator is no longer considered endangered or threatened.

The history of the American alligator became more complicated when the fashion market began producing alligator-hide products in the mid-1800s; only then did the reptile become heavily hunted for its hide in the United States. Many populations were significantly reduced by the 1960s, so the alligator was listed as an endangered species in 1967, and in 1970 it was protected under the Lacey Act, which prohibited interstate

shipment of alligator hides. From the 1970s to the 1980s, studies conducted by state agencies in Louisiana and Florida showed that alligator numbers were rapidly increasing. In Florida the Game and Fresh Water Fish Commission received four thousand to five thousand nuisance alligator complaints each year. That number has continued to grow, with numbers reaching as high as ten thousand annually in the 1990s. As a result of the population studies, both states created nuisance control programs, which have now been established in most of the nine southern states inhabited by alligators.

Researchers in Louisiana and Florida focused on the impact of alligator harvests on wild populations. Results from their studies led to the development of state alligator management programs. Their major objectives have been to implement the concept of sustained annual harvests, emphasizing the economic, aesthetic, and ecological value of alligators as a renewable natural resource. By emphasizing these values, the respective state agencies hope to provide incentives to manage not only alligators, but also the wetland and deepwater environments they inhabit.

The pattern of fieldwork common to alligator research involving egg collection is to conduct nest surveys; map the nest locations; collect eggs, transport them to controlled environments and incubate them in captivity; and conduct night-light counts to establish hunting quotas and to monitor population trends. Throughout these steps, data are collected, such as the number and position of eggs in the nests, temperature and humidity ranges, density of eggshells, maturation times, and length and weight of hatchlings. Fieldwork is heaviest in March through October, when air and water temperatures are warmer and alligators are active.

NEST IDENTIFICATION AND VERIFICATION, LAKE JESUP,

FLORIDA, JUNE 1987

MOTHER GATOR PROTECTING NEST, ROCKEFELLER REFUGE, LOUISIANA,

JULY 1993

EGG REMOVAL AND NUMBERING, LAKE JESUP, FLORIDA, JUNE 1987

EGG TRANSPORT, LAKE JESUP, FLORIDA, JUNE 1987

Louisiana has a long and rich history in alligator research, and its cultural identity is associated with these crocodilians as well as with crawfish, affectionately referred to as "mud bugs." E. A. McIlhenny, creator of the famous Tabasco pepper sauce, was also a serious naturalist who was fascinated by alligators and most of the other coastal wildlife native to his Avery Island home. In 1934 McIlhenny first published *The Alligator's Life History*, a classic text that is still in print and used by scientists and laypersons alike in understanding this strangely fascinating carnivore. Avery Island, maintained as a private wildlife preserve but open to the public, is surrounded by water and marshlands and is the tip of a subterranean mountain of salt thousands of feet deep.

The Rockefeller Wildlife Refuge, comprising 84,000 acres, is part of the coastal marshes of southwestern Louisiana in Cameron and Vermilion parishes on State Highway 82. Originally owned by McIlhenny, the property was sold to the Rockefeller Foundation with the intent that it be donated to the state of Louisiana as a wildlife refuge. It is an important refuge because it is at the southern end of the vast Mississippi River flyway for hundreds of thousands of wintering waterfowl. The refuge also serves as an important fisheries nursery for the southwest Louisiana coast. Year-round residents such as nutrias, muskrats, raccoons, otters, minks, deer, and alligators are plentiful in the area.[44]

Ranching and Farming

Besides the capture of nuisance alligators and seasonal hunting or "cropping," there are alligator ranches and farms. In ranching eggs are collected from the wild; in farming adult alligators are bred in captivity. Ranching produces the higher economic yield because alligators produce more eggs in the wild than in captivity.[45] For the highest productivity, eggs collected from the wild are raised in captivity, where predation of the eggs and the young is greatly reduced if not eliminated. Research indicates that the growth rate (based on survival of eggs and young to adulthood) is higher

in captivity than when eggs are left in the wild throughout their development, where clutches are subject to raids by predators. On ranches eggs are incubated in optimal conditions. The rancher has a larger crop of gators to raise, and more baby gators survive to one year of age; therefore yearlings are available from which to take a percentage where restocking the natural habitat is practiced, such as in Louisiana.

On ranches alligators are raised to harvesting age in houses with controlled temperature and humidity. As they get larger they are transferred to growth

ponds. In both cases the gators are fed regularly with highly nutritional feed, so they grow faster than animals in the wild. On average an alligator raised in captivity grows one and a half to two feet a year as opposed to six inches a year for a wild juvenile alligator.

In the past the most valued alligator skins have been from alligators four to five feet long. Changing husbandry practices and market demands, however, influence the length of animals harvested on ranches. Smaller animals have smaller scale patterns in the hide, so their skins

are more refined. Younger gators generally have been in fewer fights, so the
skins are not as scarred. In 1994–95
demand for small skins to satisfy a surge
in watch-strap manufacture spurred the
slaughter of alligators averaging three
feet. Thus ranches and farms mostly process gators of an average length determined by market demand for skins, with
meat production a secondary consideration.

Alligators on ranches and farms are
slaughtered every year to generate ongoing income and to make room for new
hatchlings. To reduce crowding, older and

larger alligators, which require more
space to minimize fighting and stress, are
sold or put outside in growth ponds during their final spring and summer. The
growth ponds permit raising larger alligators over several years if higher meat
yields and larger-patterned skins are
desired.

The slaughter and processing procedure is similar to that of the hunts because it is based on the same principles—to preserve the quality of the meat and skins. The gators are stunned by a blow to the head, the spinal cord and brain stem are severed, and the carcasses are kept cold until processing. The time between slaughter and skinning varies from minutes to twelve hours.

To assess the feasibility of commercial alligator ranching in the southern aquatic environment, both Louisiana and Florida conducted extensive research programs.

Participants who cooperated in a broad research effort include biological research and ecological management specialists from state agencies, universities, private aquaculture industries, and tourism businesses. Reproduction and survival rates for young alligators were important aspects of this study. If the wild population could be shown to flourish even while nests are being robbed to stock ranches, then a system of sustainable harvest could be devised and used for commercial benefit. Thus a thesis for value-added conservation could be proposed to maintain and improve the health of the south-ern aquatic lands, using the power of aquaculture business interests to compete with the demands of the land development industry.[46]

Jane Gibson

Living by the
WETLANDS

I n fast-paced, anything-for-a-buck America, there are still people for whom lakes, marshes, creeks, ponds, and rivers mean more than money. This matters because freshwater ecosystems contain tremendous biological diversity: many species "make a living" in wetland, riverine, and lacustrine environments. It matters because these play a vital ecological role in maintaining wider ecosystem health. And it matters because some wetlands in particular, long treated as wastelands to be drained, are home to people whose worlds collectively constitute equally essential cultural diversity with the knowledge, skills, and creativity to live in fragile environments without destroying them. Some of these people live in Shellcracker Haven, a tiny frontier settlement in the Orange Creek Basin, just about where Florida's heart would be.[1]

The people of Shellcracker Haven have always made their living from Lakes Orange and Lochloosa and from the lush subtropical watersheds of Prairie Creek, the River Styx, and Hatchet Creek, all of which drain the Oklawaha River. Here they developed the necessary skills and created with their own hands those technologies needed to live well in the wetland basin. They gathered Spanish moss for furniture stuffing, seined bluegills, shellcrackers, and bream for the "northern" markets of Jacksonville and parts of Georgia, put out trotlines baited with shrimp for catfish, gigged frogs, and hunted and skinned alligators.

The diversity of work in Shellcracker Haven reflects a combination of local adjustments within the ecosystem to seasonal variation in resource availability and adjustments to variation induced by politicians from the state's capital. Such diversity also points up the inherent flexibility of a self-directed workforce made up of family members. It is both the nature of their businesses and local tradition that organize extended kin and households

1. Shellcracker Haven is a pseudonym, as are other place-names and personal names, used to protect the privacy of the community. The story, however, describes true events and real people from the town whose name is taken from a fish (called locally a shellcracker) for which the lakes of Orange Creek Basin are known.

into social and economic relationships; it is the local social economy that ties them to the wetland and the lake.

Shellcracker Haven's families mold their lives and lifeways to the basin and to the world in which it is embedded. The basin is part of their heritage and part of who they are today. This place shapes individuals, presents them with challenges, and locates them in the social milieu of kinship and mutual support. In this reciprocal relationship, Shellcracker Haven's children learn meanings and values for their world that include, but go beyond, profitability. Their parents vest them with powerful incentives—a sustainable livelihood balanced with love and respect for place—to stay, work, and raise another generation beside the lake.

Ancestors of today's community came by horse- and mule-drawn wagons to the piney woods and cypress swamps more than 150 years ago. These yeoman farm families grew their own food in fertile basin soils and taught their children the values of hard work and family loyalty. Some supplemented farming with occasional fishing and hunting before the railroad made marketing cash crops both possible and desirable. Others used their success at sharecropping to buy a position in the commercial freshwater fishing industry. When the Great Depression squeezed most of the town's small farms out of business, commercial fishing and trapping became mainstays of the community's social economy and a primary source of identity for those with the fortitude and determination to carry on the tradition.

Outsiders knew the town as a fishing village at the turn of the twentieth century, and it remained so identified until in recent years people came to associate Shellcracker Haven with its alligator hunters. For the past fifty years catfish and alligators, the two primary "staples" of the local extraction economy, have most tenaciously bound the people of Shellcracker Haven to the marshes and deepwaters of the lake. Both catfishing and alligator hunting developed from the town's early history in seining various species of scaly fish, or panfish as most people there know them. Seiners took up catfishing and alligator hunting in response to conservation policies that periodically called for local adjustment to the changing availability of freshwater resources.

Commercial fishing on Shellcracker Lake began in the late nineteenth century when the Peninsular Railroad built a spur line to the water's edge. At night, when the air cooled and years of experience taught locals that fishing would be the most rewarding, kindred fishermen went to work in teams of two or three. The men tied one end of a great net to a tree or to a fishing boat and stretched the seine into a semicircle back to shore. A local old-timer told a writer from a Florida sporting magazine that as a child he watched the backbreaking labor it took to pull in, hand over hand, a 2,500-yard net whose "pocket" was then transferred to the fish house. This simple wooden structure, believed to have been built by local men out of cypress cut and milled across the lake, sat at the end of a pier above the railroad track.

Inside the fish house, fishermen dispatched the occasional alligator or turtle as well as carnivorous fish such as shad and gar, packed panfish and ice into wooden barrels, and loaded them onto a waiting railroad car. Such hard work was rewarded on the weekends, when at night the fish house became a center of social life for the townspeople. Here, under the light of kerosene lamps and the influence of moonshine, fishermen built their rowdy reputations for fist- and gunfights over cards, old insults, and women. Betsy, now in her mid-sixties, reminisced about those times:

> This boat landing down there had this old building on it. I was allowed to go down and fish, as long as the fishermen were not working down there, because it was right directly in front of my parents' place and they could see what I was doing. . . . But on Saturday night and Sunday, the fish house was off limits to any of the children because this was where the men gathered up. They had their drinks and their poker parties, and sometimes they had some rough times down there.

Naomi's daughter, Norma, grew up with Betsy. Together they sometimes hung around the fish house, playing in small wooden boats or dangling bamboo poles from the dock into the tea-colored water.[2] Betsy's mother taught her how to bait a hook and take turtles, speckled perch, or whatever "bit" off her line, and the two girls mined the waters of Shellcracker Lake for "all the bream you could want."

During the Great Depression, the lake's centrality in the lives of fishing families took on a new dimension. Cash, and most everything else, became scarce in Shellcracker Haven, so fishing families traded with local farmers: fish in exchange for eggs, milk, and a few vegetables. They also bartered with turpentiners for greens from the gardens of the "still quarters," a company-owned neighborhood within Shellcracker Haven. And turpentiners traded tools and certain staples they bought on credit at the company commissary. Trade, as it has functioned at the local and regional levels throughout human history, socially integrated the community and brought people together in new relations of mutual support. As a result, the depression worked little hardship on most families of Shellcracker Haven, who hardly noticed when it was over because of the generalized self-sufficiency brought about by necessity and a community ethos. Naomi, a woman now well into her nineties, tells this simple allegory about her exchange with a hungry child from the quarters.

2. Tannins give tea its color and also account for the color of Shellcracker Lake. Tannins are a natural by-product of cypress and other highly acidic plant "litter" that falls into the lake and breaks down there.

He wasn't a very big boy [who] come up here one evening. We had a fish box in back; we bought fish and sold them. This little boy come up to me one evening and said, "Mrs. S., do you have a fish I could buy for fifteen cents?" and I said yes. I didn't have, but I said, "Yes, I know I could find you one." He went on running round the house and I opened the fish box and reached in there and got him two. I didn't even put them on the scales.

The pennies per pound earned by local fishermen never brought the great wealth their ancestors hoped it would, but seining fed the children and kept a roof over their heads. It also gave men a way to earn the respect of their families and other fishermen, as well as recognition from outsiders who came to identify them as hardworking men with specially developed skills. To be a successful seiner, a man had to know how to build a boat and repair it. He had to know how seasons, wind and rain, and time of day could affect a harvest. He had to learn to "smell the beds" where large schools of fish spawned. And he had to know how to negotiate with the "fish dealers." These middlemen opened the door to the market for local fishermen whose labor and supply of fish they captured by providing nets and other equipment on credit.

Ironically, the improved economy associated with World War II brought about a rising tide of tourism on which the local social economy of fishing ran aground. Developers and land speculators had always advertised the area's remarkable hunting and fishing, and fish camps grew up all around the lake. Some of the sport fishermen who came on vacation year after year became retired lakefront property owners. Among them, one newcomer family claimed exclusive rights to the pier and its fish house, an action interpreted locally as a serious threat. No one back then owned a wheeled boat trailer to pull behind the requisite pickup truck, so in this time of extraordinary trust and cooperation nearly everyone in Shellcracker Haven who seined for a living kept a boat tied to the landing. Without the landing and the fish house fishermen would be out of business.

This dispute was resolved in a court battle during which Betsy's father, a respected former commercial fisherman himself, testified that the pier had traditionally been shared by members of the community. Then his heart failed and he died on the witness stand. In the wake of such catastrophe, the judge ruled in the fishermen's favor that the dock would remain public property. This decision only temporarily secured the livelihood and lifeway of the people of Shellcracker Haven. The attitude of the property owner who tried to purge the lake of commercial fishermen foreshadowed the inevitable transformation of the community and its social economy.

The complaint of sport fishermen against the seiners was an old one with a discernible ten-year pattern. The sport fishers of the eighties—1880s, that is—claimed the fishing was not as good as it was in the 1870s; those in the 1930s claimed the same with reference to the better 1920s, and so on into the 1990s. The obvious explanation, as far as sport fishermen were concerned, was and is commercial fishing, in spite of empirical, peer-reviewed, and successfully replicated biological evidence to the contrary. The politics of this battle, fought angrily in Florida's newspapers, have shaped decisions made by resource managers ever since.

In the early 1940s, 98 percent of all revenue for freshwater fish and wildlife management in Florida came from sport fishing licenses. Under tremendous political pressure from the Florida Wildlife Federation and a genuine need to improve the effectiveness of resource conservation, the Florida Game and Fresh Water Fish Commission (FGFC) sacrificed all but large-scale seining on the state's largest lakes. For its part of the bargain, the Federation agreed to throw its weight behind a state constitutional amendment that gave the FGFC regulatory authority and autonomy, immunity from legislative caprice, and the financial security necessary to carry out its conservation mandate. All the FGFC had to do was agree to eliminate commercial fishing with a proscription against seining.

As with all such Faustian bargains, the FGFC purchased its new power at a price. In a letter addressed to the agency's chief fisheries biologist, the owner of a sport fishing business threatened the agency's future and the biologist's job: "Jack, use what brains you have, keep your prestige, your job. This is a Sportsmen's State, it is the funnel of our United States. A Sports fisherman's dollar is a hundred times more valuable than a Commercial Fisherman's dollar. . . . Don't sell [short] the Florida Wildlife Federation—who created our Game and Fresh Water Fish Commission."

In the end, the Federation won control of FGFC appointees, who forced the fisheries biologist to resign. The price paid by Shellcracker Haven was even higher. Eddy Knight remembered that in the late 1940s and early 1950s as many as thirty people seined full time, which meant that half of Shellcracker Haven had come to depend on commercial fishing. The story goes that some of the seiners painted their boats black when they got the news that the tradition their grandfathers and great-grandfathers had passed down to them had become illegal. Under cover of darkness these fishermen hid "behind the hill," where they continued to practice the one thing that identified them with their proud heritage and that would support their families. But such risky activity could go on only until the newfound security and fiscal solvency of the FGFC was translated into a growing and increasingly effective enforcement branch.

Officers learned to identify the unusual carriage of a Georgia-bound car whose trunk contained hundreds of pounds of fish and ice. The law permitted them to confiscate the car, the fisherman's boat, his net, and any other equipment used to carry out illegal seining. Soon the costs outweighed the benefits. Even Charlie Knight, known affectionately by the FGFC as "a great pirate," had to give it up. With proscriptions on seining, the short-lived at-

Processing

Once a gator is killed—whether it is wild, comes from a ranch or farm, or is a nuisance gator—it is ready to be processed. The general misconception is that the alligator industry is male dominated, but women usually control the processing end. Entering processing sheds, it is usual to see women workers processing the meat and sometimes skinning the alligators or teaching the more recent hunters the skills of the trade. Violet Crews and Mary Warden, for example, have been prominent skinners and processors in Florida, since even before the Lacey Act of 1900 was amended in 1970 to protect reptiles in addition to mammals and plumed birds. During the years when alligator hunting was illegal, Violet and Mary skinned and processed nuisance gators for the state's contracted hunters. Many of the younger hunters, hunting during the alligator hunting season since the mid-1960s, do not know how to butcher their own alligators as their predecessors did.

tempt at "bootlegging" panfish left many families in the middle of what one man referred to as "the starvin' time."

Such changes, however, did not necessarily mean community disintegration, at least not for those whose stability historically depended on a strategic combination of flexibility and diversity. Even when seining constituted the most important part of the economy, men, women, and children took advantage of other opportunities as they arose. Shellcracker Haven's men hunted several species of game animals, some of which could be sold for their furs and most of which could be eaten. Stella and her son euthanized frogs and cats used by a biologist for his research. Citrus grove owners hired men and older boys to harvest fruit and prune orange and grapefruit trees. Boys worked in a town within walking distance, where they built crates to pack the celery produced on Mr. Hillcrest's muck farm. And some of their mothers and sisters weeded and picked Ford Hook lima beans and yellow squash in season.

Still, no other line of work contributed as much to households and to the community as catfishing with trotlines, even though the trotline method reduced the catch to a fraction of what families had earned with seines. Trotline fishing also changed the requirements of production and so, too, the social relations of fishing and kinship. Seining required cooperation between kinsmen from different households; catfishing shifted the responsibility to the immediate family. Women took on the important tasks of "racking boxes" and baiting hooks.[3] (Cindy only half joked that David would not marry her until she proved she could rack a box.) Men in the early years used a "launch" in late evening to put out trotlines on Shellcracker Lake. Before dawn they returned to bring in the catch and carefully laid the barbed lines in a pan from which their mothers, wives, or daughters would rack and bait them again during the day. But because the shift to catfishing meant a severe reduction in income, families intensified other activities, especially gator hunting, to compensate.

No one really knows to what extent gator hunting contributed meat to the diets and skins to the economy of Shellcracker Haven's households before experimental hunting for the state began in 1981. Up until 1943, the year the FGFC outlawed freshwater seining in the Orange Creek Basin, alligator hunting was legal and unregulated, and not very important to conservationists, developers, or wetland social economies. Still the knowledge and skills,

Jane Gibson

Living
by the Wetlands

---

3. Each "box" is actually a stack of perhaps eight to ten square trays, each containing closely spaced notches that hold the hooks of a long trotline. A woman carefully feeds the hooked line into each tray, placing each hook on the outside of a notch with loose line between hooks on the inside. When one tray is filled, she places the next tray on top of it, continuing the process until the line is "racked." Baiting each hook completes the process. When a fisherman "puts out trotlines," the baited box sits on a freely rotating spindle at the back of a boat so that the line can be slowly and carefully fed into the water from its anchor, a tree on shore or perhaps a submerged tree branch near the water's edge.

like those for other basin resources, were passed down from generation to generation to become part of a diverse and flexible strategy. Charlie Knight, the best known among the town's alligator trappers, began hunting as a teenager in the early 1940s.

> Well, I started alligator hunting when I was sixteen or seventeen years old, and I've been doing it off and on. Me and Buck done some hunting. When everybody else was failing to get gators, we'd get us three or four every night. Lot of people think it's skill, but it was just luck. I watched my wife's daddy skin when we were kids, and I watched my daddy skin. I knew it had to be real tedious, 'cause if you cut holes in the hide, that's a third of the price off.

During these early years of legal trapping, hide buyers, like fish dealers, held the upper hand. With a near monopoly on tanning, buyers could undervalue hides and fix prices at low levels. Charlie remembers selling one large hide for $2.50 a foot because the buyer claimed the skin was "buttoned." Buttons are osteoderms, bony growths in the hide that reduce the number and size of the pieces of exotic leather available for finished products.

In 1943, in response to a drop in the reported alligator harvest, the FGFC closed the breeding season and limited legal size to a minimum of four feet. In 1954, believing the population had rebounded, the agency raised the size limit to six feet. The harvest records that alarmed the FGFC about species decline in the 1940s are now known to have been incomplete. And the appearance of a population rebound in the next decade resulted from a combination of significant wetland drainage in the state throughout the 1950s and the development of "swamp buggies" that limited the natural protection available to alligators. No one questioned the validity of the early findings, and alligator season ultimately closed altogether. In 1967 the United States Fish and Wildlife Service added alligators to the endangered species list.

Just as the Volstead Act of 1919 made black-market moonshine an even more profitable, albeit risky, venture and proscriptions on seining drove up the price of bootlegged panfish, outlawing alligator hunting raised the value of alligator hides. Charlie Knight never poached an alligator, but others in Shellcracker Haven did. One man told of hunting alligators at night, taking them into the weeds to skin them, and abandoning the carcass, including the meat, at the site. Sometimes, he said, he would use the meat to bait his catfish boxes. Then he arranged a clandestine meeting with a hide buyer who, in spite of the higher prices illegal hides could command, retained control over the negotiation. It was this undependable and unpredictable situation that made seining panfish before 1943, and catfishing with trotlines afterward, the more attractive work in Shellcracker Haven.

Between 1965 and 1971, records indicate that Florida trappers sold 140,000 illegal alligator hides, a figure that, in retrospect, demonstrates the species was not endangered. When passage of the 1971 Lacey Act effectively stopped the black-marketing of alligator hides, public complaints increased about alligators in swimming pools, golf course ponds, backyards, and anywhere else they were not wanted. By the mid-1970s, the FGFC received between four and five thousand complaints annually. In response, alligators moved off the endangered species list and onto the threatened list, and the FGFC established its statewide Nuisance Alligator Control Program in 1978. Among other highly skilled trappers and skinners around the state, the FGFC hired Charlie Knight to handle the problem.

Charlie and his son David answered a complaint from an enclave of house-lined canals off Little Lake Santa Fe where two large alligators had been sighted. Some residents worried about the nearness of the toothy carnivores, whose diets were reported to include small dogs and children. As he was carrying out the search for the offending gators, an elderly resident surprised Mr. Knight when she swam by in the canal. This, she explained, was her daily routine: to swim out of the canals into the lake and back into the canals every evening. Mr. Knight reminded her that alligators begin feeding about dusk and that she would not stand a chance in the water against a hungry six-foot male. He had lost a finger to such an alligator that he mistakenly thought he had killed.

What most urban Floridians regard as nuisances (with the exception of this determined woman) turned into a boon for Shellcracker Haven. Nuisance hunting provided additional income year-round to the Knights' extended family of skinners, deboners, and meat processors. Together they saved enough money from hide sales to upgrade "the skinning shed" in anticipation of the opening up of the alligator meat market. This relationship with the FGFC paid off for the rest of the town's hunters when the state began its experimental hunts in 1981.

Orange Creek Basin and its community of experts became the FGFC biologists' cultural ecology laboratory. Here the FGFC could study the relation between hunting practices, alligator processing and marketing, and the biological cost to the alligator populations of Lakes Orange and Lochloosa. In short, researchers could determine a sustainable harvest rate that would benefit hunters, who in turn would have an economic incentive to protect the long-term viability of alligators and their habitats.

Shellcracker Haven's hunters understood the benefits of working with the FGFC after years of dealing with wily hide buyers. In exchange for state intervention into the hide market, the hunters taught the biologists everything they knew about hunting techniques, skinning, and all the ways the market and the law could be subverted. When the experimental hunts were concluded, fourteen hunters from Shellcracker Haven had earned more than $262,000 over the seven years of the project. On average this meant an additional $2,700 per household each year that could help meet basic needs.

Violet Crews and her husband live on the famous St. Johns River in Florida, where Violet operates Crews Processing House, where in May 1993 she told about the history of her processing business. Originally from Plant City, Violet lived with her former husband at Brown's Landing, also on the St. John's River. When he died, there were too many memories of him and the hard work and improvements they had achieved together.

I was at the beauty shop just up the road, asking if there was any place for sale, because I was looking for another place on the river. Peggy Tucker said she had her *place up for sale. I loved it from the time I saw it.*

I wish you could be here on the full moon. Then this is the most beautiful place in the world. I know there are beautiful places, but let me tell you something! We have as pretty sunsets here as anywhere else.

This house is about sixty years old. During that time, we've kept people when they were down and out. And they love it too. . . . That's what I said, this is the heart of my heart.

In October 1993, Violet celebrated her twenty-fifth year of living on the St. Johns River in her "heart of hearts" home and business.

Violet came to processing gators by accident. Until then, her business had been solely a well-known fish-processing operation. One day a trapper who was unhappy with another processor brought in an eight-footer. She and Diane Bowen, who still works with Violet, skinned and butchered it by trial and error. Word of their success spread. Soon a ten-footer was brought in, and they thought, What's two more feet? "Well," Violet remembered, "two feet is a big difference." They could not lift the much heavier gator onto the skinning table. "We laughed, we laughed, and we laughed, trying to get that gator on the table." They got help from a neighboring fisherman and told him to bring some backup. It took five people, because the gator weighed more than three hundred pounds!

"There is a *lot* of work processing a gator. You get about two hundred pounds of meat out of a six-hundred-pound gator. At the business's peak we did a hundred gators a season. A twelve-footer was the largest. We had A-1 meat. . . . Alligator meat is pretty white meat. The legs are dark, but most all is pretty white meat, beautiful meat." Asked about the importance of alligator processing to her family, Violet responded that it was "very important, because we weren't dressing any catfish at that time, and my husband wasn't working then." Their annual family income came from catfish, gator processing, and shrimping.

It used to be that we shrimped in the summer months. But they cut shrimping out in this area, so alligator processing was almost our full income. . . . It's hard work, and it's nasty work. We've taken hoses and hosed the whole shed down. I've come out of that door puking, because of that odor. Junior Weldon was on one side of the porch and I was on the other side, puking. . . . Diane, it didn't bother her. She would cut the stomach open, discovering what was in it—a deer, crawdads, fish, a pond scoggin [white or blue heron],[47] a coon, and a snake. We were warned when we cut into the stomach to be careful about rattlesnakes. Their fangs could be dangerous. . . . Alligators have been around me all my life. I sure didn't think I'd ever clean any alligators, but I've seen them all my life. . . . They'll lay in the water with their mouths open. There's little tinklets in their mouths that look like worms, so the fish will swim right in. That's how they get their primary source of food.

Violet describes the alligator processing industry as "very heavily regulated. . . . You do not come in here and pick up a knife unless you are OK'd by the Game Commission. The yield is about one-third meat to body weight, and most of the meat is sold to restaurants."

No matter what Violet expected in her life, now she is identified as an expert alligator processor—a legend in her own time. Her knowledge of alligators is broad, ranging from research techniques used by scientists during the night-light counts, conducted to establish hunting quotas for the coming year, to idiosyncrasies of working with alligators during and after the hunt.

I wish I could remember to tell you which way a gator rolls when he's dead. Whenever you shoot him, if he rolls one way, he's not dead; if he rolls the other way, he's dead. The way I learned that is one morning we got a big gator out of the cooler, and he was still alive. We thought he was dead and we heard that if he rolls a certain way when he's taken, then you know he's dead. I know that sounds like a phony story. I don't care. Mother Nature has its way. It's God's will for things like that to be.[48]

Gator hunting also redefined and affirmed the community's identification with hunting and fishing in the basin. It recreated the social life of the fish house in the skinning shed, though continuous work by women, men, and older children of extended families took the place of poker parties and moonshine. On some days during alligator season, one can find four generations in the Knights' skinning shed, and only the youngest are not working. The day begins early when Charlie and his son-in-law go to the cooler to select a chilly gator from the previous night's hunt. If the gator is large—and more often than not the skills and luck of these hunters produce good sized ones—it takes two strong men to carry the carcass into the shed and hoist it up onto a freshly washed stainless-steel table.

The shed comes alive with morning conversation and "Cokola." Two toddlers in a playpen in the corner watch and listen to the rapid and rhythmic *kish*, *kosh*, *kish*, *kosh* sounds of blades against whetstones. Skinning begins with the precision of a surgeon as Charlie, like his father and father-in-law before him, carefully cuts the tissue that binds the valuable hide to the body. From below, standing at his granddaddy's knee, four-year-old Bo makes engine noises with his toy airboat and asks questions about the alligator whose legs dangle from the table within his reach. The other skinner is his daddy; the deboner is Bo's uncle; and the four women who wait patiently to receive the meat they will filet are his grandmother, mother, aunt, and cousin.

After the skin is removed, Charlie stops with the hide draped across his arms and poses for a photographer. His son carries the naked gator to a second stainless steel table where Charlie's son-in-law separates meat from bone. The first pieces, white meat from the tail, will significantly increase the family's income now that "gator tail" has become popular at restaurants and Florida's million-dollar theme parks. The women of the family efficiently remove gristle and membranes and slice the large slabs of meat into filets. They are conscientious and proud of their work, just as the skinners are, and they know the meat they process is preferred by their biggest buyer.

Bo's aunt feeds each smaller piece into the tenderizer and weighs out five-pound portions. Bo's mother wraps and boxes them and seals and labels each with the official tag number of the alligator it was taken from. The meat is then hard frozen and can be sold long after gator season has passed. Red meat, mostly from the legs, goes into boxes and the freezer as well and becomes part of the family's diet.

The efficiency of this family operation is in no way compromised by continuous conversations or by the numerous visitors who stop by for a chat and a look in the cooler. Everyone catches up on everyone else's health, local gossip, and the guest speaker anticipated for the church reunion; trappers talk about how choppy the water was last night so that hunting disappointed them; the auto mechanic, also a kinsman, comes in to arrange a trade for his services; and all discuss the new rules the FGFC might implement next year. They are a family, joined to each other by blood and marriage and to the wetland by a heritage of production, pleasure, and an attachment to place. So strong is this attachment that when a large corporation tried to build condominiums on the lakeshore, the alligator hunters and catfishermen got involved and persuaded the County Commission to deny the permit.

Things changed for Shellcracker Haven after 1987 when the FGFC completed its hunting experiments. Beginning in September 1988, the FGFC initiated annual public hunting in which participants are chosen by lottery. With ten to twenty thousand applicants in the pool, Shellcracker Haven's experienced trappers stand little chance of being drawn, and a few local trappers find themselves surrounded by cigar-smoking "polyester suits" from as far away as Miami who come to hunt alligators in Orange Creek Basin.

Charlie Knight laughed as he told the story of an inexperienced hunter who asked his opinion of hunting gators from a canoe using bow and arrow. He savored the delicious irony that the ban on alligator hunting in the 1960s also meant loss of certain specialized skills among Florida's hunters. Only a few can make their own bang sticks, the weapon of choice that fires a bullet directly into the skull of an alligator from the distant end of a long handle. Only a few know the geography of the lake and the behavior of alligators. Only a few families retain the collective skills to skin and process hides and meat.

As they have always done, the families of Shellcracker Haven adjusted and added two new income-earning strategies to their repertoire. Some became "agents" paid to guide novices in the ways and places of alligators. Those with skinning sheds sold their processing skills and space in their coolers for storage of perishable carcasses. The Knights set their prices in the local tradition of face-to-face negotiations. In exchange for an undamaged, highly marketable hide, some hunters traded the alligator meat, for which the Knights received up to six dollars a pound. Other hunters paid the family up to twenty dollars a foot for their well-honed skills.

Every year now, when the public hunt has ended, the money earned on the lake and in the skinning shed pays for many things: repairs to boat motors and washing machines, school clothes for the kids, and trips to the dentist or the health clinic. Men of Shellcracker Haven then move on to take advantage of the next season's opportunities: bass fishermen pay top dollar for "shiners," a bait fish locals take with cast nets and sell to fish camps around the lake; deer season takes up much of every fall and winter into January; and they always make time for catfishing at pennies a pound.

Visitors today can still see women sitting under the shady canopies of live oak and slash pine, racking and baiting trotlines while men gather outside the skinning shed after the last catch is in the freezer. Seated on crates, they discuss plans for the next hunting season, tell stories and laugh at each other's jokes, and share information on the best places to fish and hunt gators. Not surprisingly, favorite places are seldom far from home.

A number of scholars in recent years have expressed concern that the

The hunters attach tags to the alligators' tails as soon as they are taken. Each tag has a number registered with the state agency and used by law enforcement internationally as a way to trace the legal flow of alligator products. On record are the alligator's sex and length, where the animal was caught, and the amount of meat processed. The total weight is figured based on a formula of 25 to 30 percent meat yield for wild gators, so as not to require each hunter to have scales able to hoist large alligators. The number on the tag identifies the animal throughout the tanning and sale processes. The skinner has to cut care-fully around the tag to make sure it remains secure and intact.

Transporting and processing alligators is heavy work. When a large animal is caught, it takes several people or a tractor hoist or crane to handle the volume. The nuisance alligator captured by LeRoy Overstreet, as described earlier, was taken in Marengo County, near Sweet Water, Alabama, and had to be transported a good sixty-five road miles north to Epes for processing. The animal was a male with an unskinned carcass length of ten feet, seven inches, weighing 370 pounds.

very process of commodifying natural resources leads to unsustainable resource exploitation. One explanation lies in the way we learn to think about elements of the natural environment as potential products. Instead of complexes of interwoven, living, life-supporting ecosystems, we come to see tropical forests, for example, as the raw material of hardwood furniture, bioengineering, pasture, or cash crop production. These products require cutting down the forest. In the same way, freshwater ecosystems may be drained for the land or minerals underneath. So it is important, maybe even crucial, that within many threatened ecosystems there are people who still assess environmental value in terms beyond the marketplace. Ironically, these people seldom figure in political debate, in resource management models, or in plans for resource extraction, yet it is they who know how to live in their environments without destroying them.

Bo's daddy said one day, as he rolled up a salty alligator hide and placed it in a barrel, "Someday Bo's gonna make a good gator hunter, if there's any huntin' left." This trapper knows that Florida's historical development has followed a "drain the swamp" philosophy pitted against a natural resource conservation strategy based on exclusion of people from state-managed ecosystems. But the hunters and fishers of Shellcracker Haven have demonstrated that they are as firmly rooted in their wetland as the moss-bearded bald cypress trees that shade the lake's marshy fringe. It is they who know and love this humid, subtropical world of cypress, palmetto, and water hyacinth. It is a world shared by wild hogs, deer, and camouflaged hunters in pickup trucks; by shellcrackers and shiners, and fishermen in johnboats and skipjacks; by frogs and alligators and families of alligator trappers, skinners, deboners, and meat cutters. It is a world shared by women who teach their daughters and granddaughters how to rack and bait fish boxes and by barefoot boys who laugh and splash in the shallows with cast nets, toy airboats, and fishing poles. It is people like those of Shellcracker Haven, whose lives and lifeways are fully integrated into wetland, riverine, and lacustrine environments, and it may be up to such people to sustain these fragile, essential, and elegant ecosystems.

1 4 9

Jane Gibson

Living
by the Wetlands

Once a gator is killed, the entire animal must be chilled as soon as possible to prevent the meat from spoiling. Cooling sheds are used to preserve quality. Before processing, the gator's skin is scrubbed with a chlorine-based cleanser such as Comet to remove bacteria that could contaminate the meat. The meat must be skinned, deboned, and defatted, cut into manageable portions, packaged, and frozen. Each box of frozen alligator meat is sealed and labeled with the name and address of the processor, the harvest tag number assigned at the time of capture, a box number, the weight and cut of the meat, and the date the animal was processed.

Skinning an alligator is a difficult and delicate craft. An alligator's skin is thick. Most skinners use small knives that are easy to grip and very sharp. A smaller blade permits precise cutting without puncturing the hide, which reduces its sale value. The hardest area to cut is under the legs where they join the body— also the most valuable part of the skin. This section, because of its curvature and smaller scale pattern, is used to make the toe of a boot or shoe.

In 1993, in Epes, Alabama, LeRoy and June Overstreet worked together skinning the Sweet Water nuisance gator, using the "belly method" most commonly employed by processors. This method splits the hide lengthwise high up on the sides, leaving intact the full belly, legs, tail, and throat. The "hornback method," which splits the hide down the center of the belly, flaying the whole animal out flat, leaves the scutes in the middle of the back. Such skins from small alligators are used to make pocketbooks that feature the raised scute ridge. Some hornback methods cut over one jowl, leaving the whole throat section in one piece and therefore big enough to make small items like wallets.

After the skins are removed and the meat is packaged, the heads and feet will be cut from the carcasses to make curios, and the rest will be ground for fish food, leaving only remnants of the alligator—like a tail scute section—bits hard to market. The hides are salted, rolled, and stored until auctioned. At auction these "green" skins are sold to tanners who finish the hides, tanning, scraping, dyeing, and polishing to transform them into the array of differently colored and surfaced leathers desired by the various domestic and international markets for exotic products.

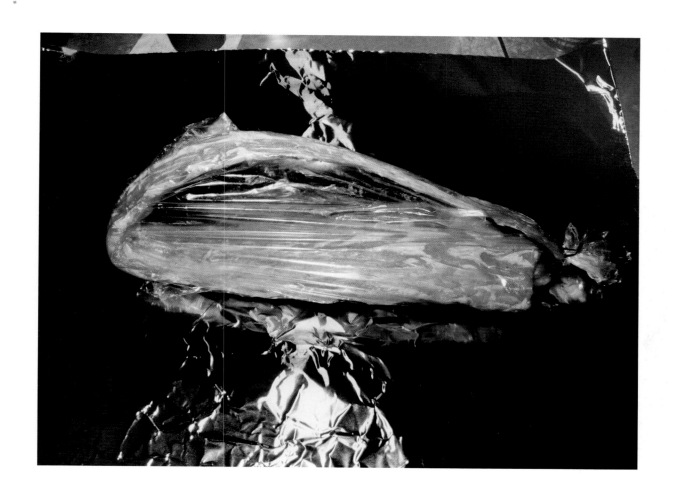

▯▮▯▮ Alligator

Big Alligator is a living legend in Florida's evolving mythology. This gator was in residence for many years on Scrammy's (Clyde Hunt's) Alligator Farm near Bushnell, Florida. Currently he lives on the Big Cypress Seminole Indian Reservation. Big Alligator inspired a song by James E. Billie, chief of the Seminole Nation as well as a singer and writer of lyrics portraying the Seminole ways and the laws of nature. The lyrics of the song "Big Alligator" tell about Chief Jim Billie's personal family experiences when he and his daughter lost their dogs to alligators.

Big Alligator   *James E. Billie*

Big alligator, he's mysterious
Big alligator, he's amphibious
Big alligator, he's dangerous
But, with a big alligator
    you can be prosperous
I was raised in the swamp
    by old grandpa
We ate turtle meat,
    a fish called gar
Grandpa told me about
    panthers and bear
But most of all he told me to
    beware:

Of hul-pah-te cho-bee
Nock-sho-nitch-kee-kah

Hul-pah-te cho-bee
Oo-kun kay-ye-wah

Hul-pah-te cho-bee
Hen-nu kay-ye-wah

Hul-pah-te cho-bee
He-mah-shah che-wah

As the days of summer
    grew longer and hot
Grandpa took me
    on my first gator hunt
We pushed through sawgrass
    and willow sloughs
With a yellow-eyed dog
    in a dugout canoe

The dog started sniffin',
    somethin' in the air
Grandpa said, "Must be gator
    over there.
Better grab your knife
    and some rope.
Remember what I told you
    when you was a boy":

About hul-pah-te cho-bee
Nock-sho-nitch-kee-kah

Hul-pah-te cho-bee
Oo-kun kay-ye-wah

Hul-pah-te cho-bee
Hen-nu-kah che-che-wah

Hul-pah-te cho-bee
He-mah-shah che-wah

At the age of twelve,
    I was sure of myself
I could catch alligators
    by myself
But my dog didn't know
    what my grandpa said
He jumped in the water
    by the gator's head

Hul-pah-te cho-bee
    didn't even pause
My dog disappeared
    in the gator's jaws
I can still hear my grandpa
    saying:

Hul-pah-te cho-bee
Nock-sho-nitch-kee-kah
Hul-pah-te cho-bee
Oo-kun kay-kee-kah

Hul-pah-te cho-bee
Hen-nu-kah che-che-wah
Hul-pah-te cho-bee
He-mah-shah che-wah

[Repeat refrain]

Many years later
    I remembered that day
How that big bull gator
    swallowed my dog
Scars and pain
    haunt my life
But I've learned to live
    and I've learned to survive

With Hul-pah-te cho-bee
Nock-sho-nitch-kee-kah
Hul-pah-te cho-bee
Oo-kun kay-kee-kah

Hul-pah-te cho-bee
Hen-nu-kah che-che-wah
Hul-pah-te cho-bee
He-mah-shah che-wah

Oh Hul-pah-te cho-bee
Nock-sho-nitch-kee-kah
Hul-pah-te cho-bee
Oo-kun kay-kee-kah

Hul-pah-te cho-bee
Hen-nu-kah che-che-wah
Hul-pah-te cho-bee
He-mah-shah che-wah

Hul-pah-te cho-bee

Hul-pah-te cho-bee[49]

A Different Way

Cultural diversity extends to geographic regions within the United States. The Cajun and Creole cultures in Louisiana, with their own versions of the French Acadian language, Cajun and Creole cooking, and Cajun and zydeco music, combine as an example of a regional character. Another is the culture of the "low country" of South Carolina, Georgia, and north Florida. This region is defined as the area influenced by tidal fluctuations and known as the Carolinian biogeographical zone, the coastal marshland between the sand beaches on the sea islands and the higher ground along the southern coastline. Historically a rice-producing area, the low country is home to both Caucasians and African Americans. The language associated with the African Americans there is Gullah, and the African American people are sometimes called Geechees. The low country is identified with marshes, beaches, and swamps; rice, greens, cornmeal and grits, seafood and spicy foods, including the various versions of hot pepper jelly; and houses with shady verandas where folks can rest out of the heat of the sun in hammocks and wicker or cane-seated chairs. Another regional character, particularly identified with Florida and Louisiana, concerns the alligators that play major roles in the cultures of those states. Gator festivals are held; school curricula include sections on the alligator industry, alligator life history, and alligator lore; tourist curios feature alligators; painted alligator cutouts crawl out of billboard advertisements; and even signs on restaurants and grocery stores tout GATOR MEAT. More limited uses of alligator products include health and beauty treatments such as cosmetic oils and suntan lotions made from the fat. Alligator penises are sold to Asian markets for making aphrodisiacs, reminiscent of North Carolina colonists who used the teeth for that purpose.[50] In each instance, the way of life is different, as if each region has a different personality; blended like condiments, they are the special ingredients that create the savory culture of the American South.

Where else but in this southern aquatic lands region would one find such professional and conservation organizations as the Alligator Trappers Association of Florida, the American Alligator Council, with representatives from Louisiana, Georgia, Florida, and Texas, and the American Alligator Cycle of Protection? All three are based on the existence and continuing prosperity of the American alligator, whose range is limited to the southern states. The Alligator Trappers Association of Florida was established to represent the people who make a living hunting and trapping alligators. It is concerned with the long-range future of the alligator and its habitat as a continuing battle against encroachment from agricultural and urban use in Florida. The organization encourages consumer education and promotes alligator skin and meat products.[51] The American Alligator Council is a national group with many of the same goals that also aims to combine efforts so as to conserve the developmental and promotional resources of the southern alligator industry. The American Alligator Cycle of Protection is a conservation and educational group. It is incorporated as a nonprofit organization in Florida but directs its programs nationwide.

Fire in the Swamp is a surreal food performance of my invention that is ultimately edible. The recipe follows:

1 three-foot slender section alligator tail
1 cup white grits
1 cup coarse-ground yellow grits
3 cups blueberry puree
1 bunch asparagus
12 broccoli florets
7-9 pairs prosthetic eyes that have been painted
    with phosphorescent gel
1/4 cup brandy
4 oranges, 4 lemons, 4 grapefruit
salt
1 tbsp. white pepper
1/3 cup vegetable oil
1/4 pound butter

You will also need eight inches of thin clear string, a large charcoal or gas grill or a grate over the hot coals of a bedded wood fire, and a three-foot-long fish platter—a long, narrow serving dish with at least a one-inch depth.

Make a marinade for the alligator tail using the fresh citrus juices, gratings from the citrus peels, white pepper, vegetable oil, and salt (to an intense tasty flavor). Put the alligator tail section in a heavy or doubled plastic bag along with the marinade. As you close the bag, squeeze out the air so the juices surround the meat and stay against the flesh throughout the soaking period of three to five hours. Grill the meat over a medium-hot fire to achieve a golden brown exterior and a pink but firm interior. Alligator tail cooks similarly to veal roast.

Cook the white and yellow grits with salt in two separate pots following the instructions for each kind. When both are done but still loose, combine them and add 1/2 stick butter.

Make a standing bunch of asparagus, tied with the clear string. Steam lightly. Set aside. Steam the broccoli florets and set them aside.

When all these foods are steamed, grilled, and pureed and the coated prosthetic eyes have been charged with light, arrange them around you on a table with the platter in front for assembly.

1. Make a long, oval bed of grits to represent a sandbar shimmering in the sun (the butter will make the white and yellow corn granules shine).

2. Carefully spoon blueberry puree around the bar of grits to represent blackwater.

3. Arch the alligator tail over the bar of grits on a diagonal with the length of the platter to portray alligators in their environment.

4. On one side of the bar of grits near the end, sink the asparagus into the grits, artfully surrounded by seven broccoli florets. Arrange the remaining five broccoli florets catty-corner on the other end of the bar, on the other side of the alligator tail. These assemblages of green vegetables represent a stand of pine trees surrounded by swamp brush and grasses with another stand of swamp brush at the other end.

5. Place pairs of charged prosthetic eyes in the blueberry puree to look like alligator eyes.

6. Warm the brandy, get some matches, and turn off the lights in the room where the dish is to be served.

7. Just before you walk in, pour the warmed brandy over the alligator tail and ignite it as you carry it into the room and set it before the guests.

8. Once the fire burns out (about two to five minutes), the meat can be carved and served with the grits. Remove the prosthetic eyes to make sure they are not eaten.

This dish is best served with other interesting side dishes such as swamp cabbage salad. Extra broccoli and asparagus may also be served in bowls once the performance is completed. A good rich white wine is excellent served with Fire in the Swamp. Accompanying music can vary according to the mood, ambiance, and character desired for the meal.

Prehistoric Presence

Guessing the Alligators
at the Charles Towne Landing
Gill Holland

Guess the alligators.
In the gardens where couples marry
folks lean over the bridge: they love the mud so!
Oh they're waking up to slide our way!
Ancien régime.

Best they love your thinking it. Watch the patriarch.
Lidded, dripping, he awaits the statistical drop.
He plays the odds like an ancient boulevardier
with a gleam in his monocle:
Eighty years sez I win.

The rail creaks lunch around the noon of this century.
What's the race? Call again
in some millennium.
Memory is dynastic.
The short decades are for grandnephews and
    grandnieces
who need patience.

I'll rest and tell myself
jokes in mud. Old ones, yes, but they are very good.
Ageds appreciate like veterans.
I recall your grandfather's boot. His leg.
Second honeymoon, an old romantic, sensible brides
    must agree.
His cane is here somewhere still.

Conquests ago I caught a bird of a bride
by her starched middle, though her young gentleman
    leaned
and reached with a riding crop.
But she loved my wisdom,
wait and grow wise. Only his hand I snagged,
yet from the sound he gave his true voice too.

Mon Vieux, many
have posed on my bridge in pictures.
Senators and street cleaners, grooms and bridesmaids,
wise virgins and foolish—I'll want a bite of all yet.
This bridge of ropes lasts long
but breaks as sure. The truth will win,
even if it takes two lifetimes.

Watch him from up here. His crust is old.
We guess high, he guesses low.
There's only one guess in the mud
but long experience.[52]

⫿⫿⫿ Mutuality

When human beings and alligators live together in one habitat, each benefiting from the association, they are living in a state of mutuality. The benefits may be both physiological and behavioral. Establishing conditions that promote such relationships between two species can be of great value. Environments that foster interaction between different organisms living in close physical association demonstrate a mutually beneficial symbiosis.

In the case of humans and alligators, where one species is significantly more intelligent, part of a successful equation is for people to recognize the instinctive actions and reactions in the association and use their knowledge to mediate the relationship. The principle underlying conservation and people's sustainable use of aquatic lands and alligators is mutuality. In today's world of increasing human population mutuality is achieved through ecological stewardship—managing the environment for all living species. Stewardship means accepting the responsibility to be informed and to act for the good of the whole ecosystem.[53]

By acting on informed responsibility in management and in cohabitation, people create a state of mutuality with wild species. On a macro level mutuality is fostered through ecological conservation programs and the production, publication, and dissemination of information that helps others understand the reasons for and means of mutually beneficial cohabitation. On a micro level mutuality is fostered by personal, family, and business practices. Both macro and micro levels are needed to improve the health of our ecosystem.

Stewardship is practiced on many levels. Some conservation efforts restrict the public from using wild animal habitats. These areas are usually called "preserves." Prohibiting use of the land by people keeps the environment undisturbed so that other animals can reproduce without human interference. Other conservation areas promote interaction between people and wild species, and some permit seasonal hunting in an effort to prevent overpopulation and to cover maintenance costs. These areas may be owned by federal or state governments, corporations, or private citizens. Allocating resources and maintaining them is recognized as environmental stewardship whether the land is publicly or privately owned.

A prime example of stewardship in waterfowl management is the Gulf Coast Joint Venture, a partnership formed to pool the resources of Alabama, Mississippi, Louisiana, and Texas. This plan, created in 1986 by the United States and Canada and joined in 1988 by Mexico, is a partnership of local citizens, private companies, conservation organizations, and government agencies to attempt to offset plummeting waterfowl populations in North America by creating a state of mutuality between the people of those states and the waterfowl. It constitutes collective stewardship.

In alligator management, an example of ecological stewardship is the authorizing of seasonal alligator hunts on private lands in South Carolina to encourage maintenance of the wetlands and deepwater habitats. Another example is the use of a professional alligator specialist by Lykes Brothers Ranch to manage the alligator population on Lykes properties in south Florida. Management plans like these are strictly governed by state regulations intended to produce a positive aesthetic and ecological effect on the ecosystem. Mutuality between people and alligators exists on tangible and intangible levels in diverse habitats across the American South. Some places commonly used by humans and alligators to the mutual benefit of both are described here.

The Aransas National Wildlife Refuge
has nearly 55,000 acres of oak wood-
lands, freshwater and saltwater marshes,
and coastal grasslands. The refuge has
deer, javelinas, coyotes, bobcats, feral
hogs, and alligators among its inhabitants and provides wintering grounds for
the endangered whooping crane. Aransas,
midway between Rockport and Port
Lavaca on the Texas Gulf Coast, is part of
the Gulf Coast Joint Venture to improve
waterfowl habitat. As a refuge, not a
preserve, these lands are also designed to
let people experience landscape with
wildlife that is not easily accessible otherwise.

On both sides of Louisiana State Highway 27, headed north from the Grand Chenier road (State Highway 82) at Oak Grove, are privately and corporately owned aquatic habitats where wildlife abounds. Few people live there year-round; most dwellings are small weekend cabins used for hunting and fishing. On the interior canals the mudbanks that characterize the region are kept pushed back by heavy equipment that cleans the canals of overgrown plant life so watercraft can pass. The Louisiana mudboats used by hunters, fishers, and crawdad catchers are designed to move through mud, grasses, and weeds. These flat-bottomed boats have powerful engines high in a housing in the center of the craft. The engine turns a screw-type propeller in the back shaped so as to shed debris as it turns. Mudboats are identified with the specific character of these particular wetlands and deepwater canals and lakes.

The water bounty of this region is savored in homes, in restaurants, and at festivals. Catfish nuggets, crawfish étoufée, alligator jambalaya, shrimp creole, fried gar, crab sauce piquant, oyster burgers, and sautéed frog legs are normal fare, and there's more! While savoring delicacies at the festivals, one can listen

and dance to music from both Cajun and Creole cultures. At local festivals such as the Cajun French Music Association's Cajun Music and Food Festival in Lake Charles, accomplished Cajun musicians, often described as able to intermingle great joy and deep sorrow in the same shout or cry, award a coveted handmade accordion as a first prize to an upcoming star such as Thomas Guidry. Internationally known zydeco musician Boozoo Chaviz frequents local festivals and music bars playing bayou dance and party music, with the sound of the blues included. Both Cajun and zydeco music, learned from family and friends, are performed in bayou communities at social events and in dance halls. No wonder so much emphasis is placed on food and music in Louisiana: both hold distinctive positions of significance for American culture, born out of and nurtured by the land and the aquatic habitats.

White Rock Bluff, an eighty-foot cliff on the Tombigbee River near Epes, Alabama, is the site of Fort Tombecbe. White Rock Bluff is named for the banks of the Tombigbee, whose calcium-white slopes form a dramatic background for the basking alligators that frequent the river along with the commercial barges and fishing boats.

Fort Tombecbe was built in an area previously claimed by both France and England. The fort was founded by the French in 1699 and occupied until 1763, then was held by the British until 1768. The Spanish gained control in 1794 and occupied the site until 1797 under the name Fort Confederation. In 1802 President Thomas Jefferson issued orders establishing the site as an Indian trading house or factory called the Choctaw Trading House: Fort St. Stephens and Fort Confederation. This endeavor lasted until 1823, when the establishment was closed after Congress abolished government-owned trading businesses. It was taken over as a private business for a number of years until it was deserted. Now Fort Tombecbe's ruins stand high above the river in the countryside of west-central Alabama, identified by a marker as one of the most significant historical sites in the state.[54]

Opposite the fort site on a sunny day you might see the dark, lizardlike form of an alligator against the white banks of the Tombigbee River. Though it looks distinctly different from more typical aquatic environments, this is also alligator habitat, according to LeRoy Overstreet, who has lived along the river for more than thirty years and is a frequent visitor by water and by land. He delights in historical and vernacular accounts of his region, such as Johnny Horton's song about the Battle of New Orleans, which describes the New Orleans fracas in terms similar to the description given of the history of Fort Tombecbe.

Stewardship in other areas that have alligators, such as Mississippi and North Carolina, means hunting is not allowed. As yet the lower number of alligators in these states dictates that conservation and protection are desired but hunting is not. Aquatic habitats as far north as the Pearl River Refuge just outside Jackson, Mississippi, have alligators in their waters. Other areas near housing developments around Jackson are prime alligator habitats as well, but the number of nuisance calls is still low.

The eastern part of North Carolina is similar in its reports of alligator sightings. A twelve-foot alligator stopped traffic for an hour and a half on State Highway 133 in Brunswick County in 1994. When accosted by passersby while crossing the road, the animal just "sulled up" (balked) on the pavement. Officials found it tricky to rouse the gator and motivate it to move, but it finally crossed into the marsh.[55] Such an event is unusual in North Carolina at this time, but alligators are found in rivers farther inland than most North Carolinians suspect.

Like the history of the Everglades, that of the Okefenokee includes efforts to drain the swamp. In 1891 the Suwannee Canal Company began digging a series of canals to lead the water into the St. Marys River, intending to gain millions of dollars worth of timber and fertile land. This project was a failure, but many of the canals still exist and provide access to the interior of the swamp. Now, even without being very swampwise, you can safely walk the boardwalks or take a boat into the interior following maps and markers.

For thousands of years leaves, other dead vegetation, and decaying substances fell into the water, forming layers of peat five to ten feet thick throughout the swamp. As the bottom vegetation decays, gases form and eventually work their way to the surface, breaking loose sections of the peat bed. Seeds and dust blow over the swamp and combine with the roots of water plants to form a thick floating mass that looks like land. The thicker sections have a spongy surface that can be walked on but will rise and fall with a person's weight; thus came the Indian name Okefenokee, "Land of the Trembling Earth."

From this extraordinary swamp grew a legendary figure, Miss Lydia, born on Cowhouse Island in 1864 and self-educated. Lydia Smith was a strong woman over six feet tall, known to carry timbers the size of railroad ties on her shoulders. She was a good businesswoman and a tireless worker; beginning with a cow, a sow, and a few dollars, she turned them

into 45 acres of land, bought "dirt cheap." Some forty years later she owned nearly 30,000 acres of timber land and was known as the Okefenokee millionaire. Miss Lydia never hired an overseer: she managed her holdings herself, a familiar figure to workers as she rode her horse in full skirts, with a man's felt hat pulled down on her head.

Miss Lydia married twice, once in 1903 to D. Gordon Stone, who died in 1926; at sixty-three she married J. Melton Crews, "Doll Baby," who was forty-two years her junior. The most often repeated story about this couple is about the time Doll Baby was sentenced to thirty years in the penitentiary for murder. Miss Lydia supposedly visited a high official and got him released in exchange for a large check. Miss Lydia picked up Doll Baby, drove home, and stopped payment on the check. Whether or not this is an accurate account, he came home and stayed for good. Lydia Crews died in January 1938, leaving Doll Baby a very wealthy young widower. Miss Lydia's legend lives on.[56]

Southern lands are rich with diverse water resources. The headwaters of the Suwannee River are in the Okefenokee, as are those of the St. Marys River. The Wakulla River, designated one of the "outstanding Florida waters," originates at Wakulla Springs, one of the largest springs in Florida, and runs south for about ten miles through Wakulla County to join the St. Marks River at St. Marks, Florida. Species inhabiting the Wakulla River area include the endangered West Indian manatee, wood stork, and peregrine falcon as well as the threatened bald eagle, Florida black bear, southeastern American kestrel,

and eastern indigo snake. Species of special concern on the forest-lined Wakulla include the American alligator, gopher tortoise, limpkin, one-toed amphiuma, osprey, snail kite and swallow-tailed kite, golden eagle, Woodville Cave crayfish, and Suwannee cooter.[57]

Also in Florida is Lake Okeechobee, fed primarily by the Kissimmee River on the north and secondarily by Fisheating Creek on the west. The stories of its development—its canals and dikes, the hurricanes, floods, and droughts—all document half a century of taming a wilderness. Lake Okeechobee is the largest freshwater lake in the continental United States. As recently as 1910, the shoreline of Okeechobee was said to be among the wildest and most inaccessible regions on this continent. The story of Okeechobee is the story of one of America's last frontiers, but not one that is well known.

Lawrence E. Will, in his *Cracker History of Okeechobee*, spins the history as a yarn. Using Cracker language, he provides a sense of Okeechobee's relevance by placing it in the context of the Everglades.[58] "To understand Lake Okeechobee, son, you've got to understand the Everglades, for by nature and geography they must always go together, just like eggs must go with grits. And so you ask, what is this Everglades? . . . It was all a sea of grass, growing head high in shallow water, spread out far beyond a buzzard's ken. After the first canals were dug you'd ride all day, from the lake's custard apple belt down to New River's leafy banks, and see nothing from the boat's top deck but unbroken, endless, waving sawgrass glistening in the sun."

In another section he describes the lake in the infinite detail of a poet-naturalist. He further portrays the Native American population in Florida, the development of the water management system, the importance of catfishing on the lake, the first railroad, and much more.

Lake Okeechobee is still a haven for those who want to fish. The area around

the lake is full of fish camps where people can get a room, clean their fish or have someone clean them, and have their catch served to them for dinner in the dining room. Typical fare at a fish camp is fried fish, hush puppies with orange blossom honey, slaw, french fries, and sweetened iced tea. The best hush puppies are made with yellow cornmeal, eggs, chopped onions, salt, baking soda, and buttermilk, but *no sugar*. It's that glob of fragrant orange blossom honey on a hot, savory hush puppy that sets your taste buds singing. What a delightful experience that is!

Okeechobee's waters are also chock-full of alligators, turtles, and frogs, and restaurants around the lake feature these delicacies. Alligator hunters traditionally hunted Okeechobee's public waters and the Everglades canals south of the lake, though since 1989 only the lake waters are legal areas for gator hunting. The land around Okeechobee used to be all saw grass; now, drained, it is used mainly for sugarcane, other agricultural crops, and pasture for cattle. In the areas around Okeechobee are private lands managed to develop and maintain a healthy alligator population. Although public access is not allowed on the private lands, both Lake

Okeechobee and the Everglades provide a rich sustainable resource for alligators as hunted under Florida's guidelines.

The American alligator's highest numbers are in Florida and Louisiana. People who have lived there most of their lives generally respect the ways of wildlife and live in accord with nature. These states have vast aquatic acreages in a relatively warm and humid climate, particularly conducive to alligator reproduction and survival. But Georgia has the legendary Okefenokee Swamp, also known for numerous accounts of alligator encounters. Georgia alligator lore is colorfully related in Francis Harper and Delma Presley's *Okefinokee Album*. Historically the Okefenokee Swamp is famous for its prodigious populations of snakes, bears, insects, and alligators, but relatively few people. Life in the swamp required a strong character and a hardy constitution.

At present, people visit the Okefenokee via two parks, the Okefenokee National Wildlife Refuge, established in 1936, and the Okefenokee Swamp Park, a privately owned and maintained nonprofit organization. The Okefenokee, one of the largest and most primitive swamps in America, stretches over southeast Georgia and dips into north Florida, covering more than 600 square miles. Fed almost entirely by rainwater, it is not stagnant because its waters constantly circulate in channels throughout the swamp.

Two Rivers Ranch, at the confluence of the Hillsborough River and Blackwater Creek, northeast of Tampa, Florida, supports cattle ranching, timber operations, and recreational and residential use while carefully guarding functional natural systems. Babcock Ranch was the private land used to conduct research that resulted in Florida's Private Lands Alligator Harvest Program. Both ranches are examples of successful stewardship, having created states of mutuality.

The greatest pressure on such small natural systems is proximity to urban sprawl, which affects small conservation areas through laws, regulations, politics, and a state economy focused on promoting population growth. Private landowners who provide environmental stewardship of the ecosystem are too often encouraged or even required through eminent domain or taxation to sell their land for residential and business development or in order to provide potable water, roads, and energy sources.[59]

Today rural lands are being further split up and isolated, making it increasingly difficult to maintain viable natural systems. The ecological concerns for proper stewardship of land and natural resources represented by people like the owners of Two Rivers Ranch and Babcock Ranch frequently conflict with the more short-sighted land use and land management attitudes and practices of their commercially developed "neighbors."[60] Such conflict in the southern wetlands and deepwater habitats could be reduced by state support of an ecologically informed land ethic and policies that include sustainable use options.

An ecologically sound land ethic integrated into state development schemes and promoted through public education would help an area's citizens manage our environmentally significant lands more successfully. The land ethic assumes a dynamic and inevitable connection between the natural and human-constructed worlds, including ecological integrity and aesthetics. The land ethic gets us away from the nature versus culture mentality that pervades modern thought.

 **Deepwaters**

Florida   *Elizabeth Bishop*

The state with the prettiest name,
the state that floats in brackish water,
held together by mangrove roots
that bear while living oysters in cluster,
and when dead strew white swamps with skeletons, dotted
as if bombarded, with green hummocks
ancient cannon-balls sprouting grass.
The state full of long S-shaped birds, blue and white,
and unseen hysterical birds who rush up the scale
every time in a tantrum.
Tanagers embarrassed by their flashiness,
and pelicans whose delight it is to clown;
who coast for fun on the strong tidal currents
in and out among the mangrove islands
and stand on the sand-bars drying their damp gold wings
on sun-lit evenings.
Enormous turtles, helpless and mild,
die and leave their barnacled shells on the beaches,
and their large white skulls with round eye-sockets
twice the size of a man's.
The palm trees clatter in the still breeze like the
bills of the pelicans. The tropical rain comes down
to freshen the tide-looped strings of fading shells;
Job's Tear, the Chinese Alphabet, the scarce Junonia,
parti-colored pectins and Ladies' Ears,
arranged as on a gray rag of rotted calico,
the buried Indian Princess's skirt;
with these the monotonous, endless, sagging coast-line
is delicately ornamented.

Thirty or more buzzards are drifting down, down, down,
over something they have spotted in the swamp,
encircles like stirred-up flakes of sediment
sinking through water.
Smoke from woods-fires filters fine blue solvents.
On stumps and dead trees the charring is like black
velvet.
The mosquitoes
go hunting to the tune of their ferocious obbligatos.
After dark, the fireflies map the heavens in the marsh
until the moon rises.
Cold white, not bright, the moonlight is coarse-meshed,
and the careless, corrupt state is all black specks
too far apart, and ugly whites; the poorest
post-card of itself.
After dark, the pools seem to have slipped away.
The alligator, who has five distinct calls:
friendliness, love, mating, war, and a warning—
whimpers and speaks in the throat
of the Indian Princess.[61]

J. Whitfield Gibbons

Living with
ALLIGATORS

I n dealing with human beings and the American land ethic, being first counts for little. Alligators were in the New World long before Amerindians or Europeans arrived, and long before the region was named America. The fossil record suggests that forerunners of the alligator inhabited the North American continent sixty-five million years ago.

People's traditional attitude assumes dominion over other creatures. This attitude prevails especially when another species has biological attributes perceived as either contributing to or harming humans' well-being. The alligator, which exhibits both traits, is symbolic of the American land ethic: exploiting any natural resource is ethical if doing so might benefit or protect people.

Alligators are exceptional and outstanding. In its high profile and popular image the alligator surpasses the multitude of North American animals. Indeed, its reputation in the public mind as a top contender among native wildlife parallels those of the grizzly bear, mountain lion, and gray wolf.

Among this country's reptiles only the American crocodile shares its dual qualities of large size and complex social behavior. These two crocodilian traits alone set these two related species apart from all the over 250 species of reptiles found on the continent. Large body size and parental care, along with a dependence on wetlands, are responsible for the focus on alligators from a land-use perspective.

The alligator is distinct from the American crocodile in being widely distributed, both historically and currently, solely in the United States and primarily in freshwater systems. In fact the American alligator and the Chinese alligator, a similar-appearing almost extinct species of Asia (a victim of the Asian land ethic?), are the only two crocodilian species native to warm temperate regions. All others are restricted to tropical or subtropical areas. The crocodile's geographic range in North America is confined to the southern tip of Florida where it inhabits estuarine or saltwater habitats; crocodiles are more abundant in many parts of Central America than in Florida.

The alligator is truly North America's leviathan. Because of its distinctiveness, it serves as an ideal faunal symbol of the American land ethic. And the alligator has not lacked public notice since pre-Columbian times.

Since the earliest Americans first made camps and built villages on the shores of southern lakes, rivers, and marshes, alligators and humans have affected one another. The impact of alligators on people has been primarily psychological—based more on speculation about what a reptile the size of a small dinosaur might be capable of than on observed effects. Tangible events have also occurred, however, such as occasional attacks on humans. Less obtrusive, and not necessarily negative, effects have also resulted from habitat modification in the form of "gator holes" and dens. Even more difficult to measure has been the alligator's predation on species such as furbearers or game fish, which trappers or fishermen perceive as unfair but controllable competition.

Thus alligators can, or might be presumed to, influence the well-being of humans. And humans have traits, including a tendency to subdue other creatures and dominate the land, that affect the existence of alligators. The characteristics of both species ensure interaction of some type when individuals of the two species want to occupy the same space at the same time. Compared with most other animals that inhabit the earth, both are big, both modify their habitat in recognizable ways, and each is capable of killing the other.

Ironically, the attitude of most North Americans and the behavior of alligators relative to land and nature do not differ in one sense. Both exploit the land for subsistence without regard for sustainability. Both operate based on a creed of individual prosperity, with some allowance for charity toward their kin but often without regard for the welfare of other species or other individuals of their own kind. As a single hide hunter might poach all the alligators in a lake, so might a single alligator, given the opportunity, eat all the big fish or beavers there. Neither species shows any compunction about the "tragedy of the commons."[1]

Humans and alligators differ considerably in one respect, however. Human beings kill for sport (presumably to confirm their dominion over other creatures) or simply for trinkets and souvenirs (the tangible evidence of domination). Alligators qualify as a target for these purposes. But alligators kill nothing for sport and do not normally attack humans for food or for any other reason without provocation.

In the spirit of the American culture of development (that is, progress) any natural resource is exploitable. And any animal that can be considered a threat to people or their property draws attention to itself. If the transgressions are economically disadvantageous or indisputably injurious to human health, the species may become a target for extermination. The localized elimination of native termites by pest control agencies is one example. The

1. Garrett Harding, "The Competitive Exclusion Principle," *Science* 131 (1960): 1292–97.

regional extirpation of the *Anopheles* mosquito, the vector of malaria, is another. Even the American bison, the principal food source of the Plains Indians who were competing with European colonists for land during the nineteenth century, serves as an example of systematic eradication on a more widespread scale. An early American land ethic sanctioned removal of any species that impeded expansion of the ruling population or improvement of their status, whether spatially, numerically, or aesthetically. Neither body size nor taxonomic group was taken into consideration.

Any species that stood in the way of development or that could fulfill human needs or wants was a fair target for abolishment. Besides meeting these criteria, the alligator was subject to attack for another fundamental reason. If members of a species can be construed as a danger in a physical confrontation, their subjugation in combat may serve as certification of manhood. Any large animal that posed even a potential physical threat to humans qualified. How has the alligator been perceived in this arena, and how has the American land ethic affected its treatment? Also, has the land ethic changed over time to include concerns about ecology, community, and aesthetics?

Most reports of unprovoked alligator attacks on people are equivocal, although numerous attacks in response to provocation — albeit unwitting provocation in most instances—have been documented. Many attacks spring from alligators' powerful predisposition for maternal care. Crocodilians exhibit guarding of the young more strongly than other reptiles. Mother alligators, particularly in habitats where they are not intimidated by humans, will protect their eggs and recently born young from all predators, including people. Also, an alligator that is captured or otherwise pestered shows no restraint about biting a person. Logically the black mark should not go on the alligator's side of the ledger for such performances, but it does.

Threat displays for the protection of young, as well as individual defensive behaviors, regardless of whether anyone gets hurt, contribute to the alligator's indictment as a dangerous creature, one that does not know its proper place in a homocentric world. That dogs and horses kill more people in the United States each year than alligators have killed in any century is irrelevant. The alligator is part of the land, and the old American land ethic does not sanction survival of native species that perform pernicious acts.

Alligators will eat dogs. In one bite. Even when a person is on the other end of the leash. But as I stated in *Keeping All the Pieces*, "Is it fair to condemn an alligator that has lived for thirty years in a coastal swamp, has watched its habitat be converted into a resort, and then proceeds to eat the first poodle that walks down to the edge of the new golf course?"[2] I think not. The responsibility rests with the dog's owner to know enough about the natural surroundings not to bring a small prey animal to the edge of a lake where big

2. Whit Gibbons, *Keeping All the Pieces: Perspectives on Natural History and the Environment* (Washington, D.C.: Smithsonian Institution Press, 1993), p. 76.

carnivores survive by eating other animals. But the traditional land ethic favors human property above any entitlement of a wild species. In eating dogs, the alligator falls prey to the American land ethic by infringing on this tenet.

Nevertheless, few people familiar with the habits of alligators really consider them an unmanageable threat to humans who leave them alone. But alligators do indeed pose a potential physical danger to people, a characteristic that has led, in my view, to their exploitation for demonstrating human prowess. Justification that alligators suit this purpose has been fortified by their being enormous carnivorous opponents with big teeth and powerful jaws. The American alligator qualifies as a species for demonstrating one's manhood, an acceptable extension of the American land ethic.

One of the obvious features qualifying alligators for this role is their immense size. Adult females characteristically are six to nine feet long. Males reach maturity at a larger size; they commonly grow to about twelve feet and can weigh more than five hundred pounds. The largest alligator ever reported, in *The Alligator's Life History* by E. A. McIlhenny, was a Louisiana animal nineteen feet, two inches long.[3] McIlhenny, a name familiar to anyone who has read the label on a bottle of Tabasco sauce, also mentioned specimens from fifteen to eighteen feet, but most large alligators he noted were ten to twelve feet, the normal maximum seen now. Exceedingly large alligators, above thirteen feet, appear to be rarer today.

Perhaps this near absence of the giants of yesteryear is a consequence of the elimination of most older, larger individuals by the middle of the twentieth century. Another possibility is that far fewer adult alligators are observed in modern times than a century ago and samples are therefore less likely to include the rare enormous outliers. A final possibility, one not accepted by most alligator historians but remaining unresolved, is that the extreme sizes reported in the past were a result of unintentional misreporting or mismeasurement. Whatever the true maximum size ever attained by an alligator, twelve-foot reptiles weighing more than a quarter of a ton have always existed in the American South since human occupancy and unquestionably qualify as a challenge in a contest for dominance.

Both ends of a big alligator reinforce the challenge. A well-placed tail swipe from an adult alligator can turn a boat over in the water or break a man's leg on land. But the real threat to a human challenger is the mouth. Alligators have big teeth, and their jaw muscles are so powerful that the strongest person on earth could not pull them apart. An example of their jaw strength was given by McIlhenny, who slid a steel bar into the open mouth of a large alligator. The alligator crunched down on the unyielding bar, closing its mouth completely. The force drove two teeth upward, penetrating the animal's upper jaw. McIlhenny was able to extract the teeth by pulling them

3. E. A. McIlhenny, *The Alligator's Life History* (Boston: Christopher, 1935; reprinted Berkeley, Calif.: Ten Speed Press, 1987), p. 61.

out through the top of the jaw, after which the holes healed and the alligator survived, but with the permanent loss of the two teeth.

The American land ethic has been exercised on the alligator as a leviathan to be slain for honor since the dawn of human habitation of the continent. According to Vaughn L. Glasgow in *A Social History of the American Alligator*, "Native Americans have, of course, been wearing alligator teeth around their necks since time immemorial."[4] What other reason than to demonstrate that one is the conqueror, the other the vanquished?

Expressions of this natural, though primitive, human instinct to demonstrate physical prowess continued in postcolonial times. Among the earliest accounts of this interpretation of the early American land ethic were the shooting of basking alligators from steamboats as early as the 1820s and John J. Audubon's accounts of alligator hunting in the 1830s. A modern reenactment of this occurred in 1980 when singing cowboy star Roy Rogers took a trip to Louisiana so he could shoot his first alligator, using a pistol and with the permission of the Louisiana Wildlife and Fisheries Commission. Even today numerous records exist of individual alligators being shot and the carcasses left to rot. Such acts are now judged by most Americans to be unacceptable, but they occur because of a prevailing attitude in America that killing wildlife is an unalienable right.

The rationale in all these instances was none other than "sport," a form of amusement for people in what was once perceived as a land of endless wildlife, or a lack of concern for its demise. The American land ethic in the past included an attitude, which remains with us in much of American society today, that animals have no rights.

The American land ethic is changing in regard to treatment of individual animals in natural habitats. *Sustainability* has joined *stewardship* as part of the general public's vocabulary, is prescribed by the environmentally aware, and is acknowledged as acceptable, even desirable, by segments of the corporate world. The natural world has always operated on a sustained yield principle for its biological resources. When removal exceeds replacement rate, the supply of the commodity diminishes. And though rarity at first increases value, this stage is followed by its not being cost-effective to obtain.

The American alligator serves as the paradigm of this principle and an example of how we can go too far in our exploitation. Alligators have given Americans a second chance to prove that these impressive reptiles can be managed and respected as a natural resource. We will get no second chance with passenger pigeons, Carolina parakeets, and ivory-billed woodpeckers. And the jury is still out concerning the success of species recovery efforts directed toward wolves and panthers, whooping cranes and condors, and many other less conspicuous critters.

4. Vaughn L. Glasgow, *A Social History of the American Alligator* (New York: St. Martin's Press, 1991), p. 59.

❀ Four Views
of the Everglades

From the roof of a glades camp that hunters and scientists use alike, grasses and
vegetation are seen growing through
water as it flows from the Kissimmee River
southbound for the Gulf of Mexico and
Florida Bay. When you look in four direc-
tions within a few minutes, the changing
angles of the light alter your perception of
the landscape as you pivot from west
to south to east to northeast until your
vision includes an alligator's basking site,
identified by a drag mark in the drying
mud. This seems like a quiet scene, but
sounds are insistent—sometimes lovely,
occasionally alarming and horrific. As
you lie in the darkness on your cot, the
shriek of a bullfrog being eaten by a snake
makes your blood run cold and keeps
you ever mindful of the cycle of life and
our position in it.

Whereas certain traits led to alligators' being a target for abuse and overexploitation, others have allowed them to recover from what was presumed to be near extinction as a result of their removal from habitats throughout their geographic range. One trait is their high reproductive rate, coupled with maternal care. Another is their adaptability to living in many of the aquatic habitats designed or altered by humans. A third is their ability to remain in the presence of people unobtrusively and in many instances without extensive interaction.

The other vertebrate species mentioned above, some extinct and others extirpated from most of their former geographic range, are characterized by appreciably lower rates of replacement—they have fewer young. In addition, some were dependent on specific habitat types and had neither the ecological flexibility to adjust to changing habitat conditions nor, in the case of the large mammals, the ability to live unobtrusively near people. Had alligators not had high reproductive output and an ability to adjust to substantial habitat change, the species almost certainly would not have recovered to the extent it has. It is possible that their numbers otherwise might have diminished to levels at which extinction was inevitable.

In care and attention to their young, alligators are by human standards the best parents among North American reptiles. No other American reptile, except perhaps the American crocodile, will defend its eggs and young from large predators, including people. Some reptiles, such as most turtles, simply deposit their eggs in a nest in the ground, cover them, and return to the water without even a backward glance. The young of live-bearing snakes, including rattlesnakes and garter snakes, are on their own after parturition. Perhaps some security is afforded the offspring of a venomous species that remains in the vicinity of its mother, but its safety is purely incidental, not a consequence of active protection by the female.

Alligators also have more offspring at a time than most other reptiles or birds, and more than any North American mammal. Clutch size in an alligator nest normally ranges from thirty to forty and may be as high as sixty. This allows rapid repopulation of a habitat even when the adult population has been reduced to a small size. The rate of repopulation is affirmed by McIlhenny's report of the number killed on 174,000 acres of wildlife refuge in Louisiana where alligator hunting had been prohibited for four years. When the area was opened up for alligator removal for a single summer in 1916, the total take was 88,089 alligators, roughly 1,000 per day! As McIlhenny said, "This is illustrative of how rapidly alligators will increase if left alone."[5] This is one reason alligators, compared with some less fortunate species, survived the American land ethic of the 1800s and the first two-thirds of the twentieth century: they could steadily replace themselves if given an opportunity. Mc-

5. McIlhenny, p. 86.

Ilhenny's report also demonstrates how rapidly the alligator population in an area can be annihilated by humans.

Any land ethic is based on knowledge, or at least perception, of nature. In America the science of ecology has contributed greatly to an understanding that our environmental excesses cannot be tolerated if we are to maintain the natural world. Knowledge about the ecology and behavior of North America's largest reptile has come slowly to scientists, and many biological mysteries remain. This is not to say that some of this knowledge was not available at one time, such as among the Cajuns in Louisiana, the early inhabitants of Georgia's Okefenokee Swamp, or the Seminoles in Florida. Those who lived with alligators learned their haunts and habits. But alligators have had a significant impact on the human psyche. Sorting fact from fiction about an animal that gets three times bigger than a normal man and can crush the life out of a full-grown deer has not been an easy task for scientists.

By far the best and most thorough early account of the natural history of the alligator "has been given short shrift by zoologists," stated the late Archie Carr in his vindication of the ecological observations McIlhenny reported in his book.[6] From his salt dome in Louisiana, known as Avery Island, this gentleman chili farmer spent much of his time in casual and planned observation of these magnificent creatures of the freshwater lowlands of Louisiana, the swamps and marshes, rivers and lakes.

McIlhenny first reported some of the behavioral characteristics of alligators that made them most unusual compared with noncrocodilian reptiles — nest building, protective maternal behavior, and vocal communication. These and other traits have subsequently been used by scientists to ratify the distinction of crocodilians from other reptiles and to place the group in phylogenetic context. Some even consider the crocodilians to be closer relatives of birds than of other modern reptiles.

But McIlhenny was more than an observer of the animal itself. He also, as early as the first third of the twentieth century, was observing the demise of a fabulous beast through human actions: "That the alligator has already been exterminated over a large portion of its former habitat is a fact, and one that civilization should not be proud of." He had remarked earlier that they had "been hunted so relentlessly for their skins that they are now greatly reduced in numbers, and in many areas where they were formerly abundant are now exterminated."[7]

In the spirit of the prevailing land ethic, hide hunters of the late nineteenth and early twentieth centuries scoured the southern marshlands, swamps, and waterways from Texas to North Carolina in search of alligators that would make the best skins. Alligator shoes and purses became status

6. Archie Carr, Foreword to E. A. McIlhenny, *The Alligator's Life History* (Boston: Christopher, 1935; reprinted Athens, Ohio: Society for the Study of Amphibians and Reptiles, 1976), p. v.
7. McIlhenny, pp. 116 and 25, respectively.

symbols representing money and class in the United States and abroad. Alligator leather products of other sorts were also marketed. None were defined as necessary; they were primarily curiosities that cost a lot of money. Not that the hide hunters themselves got wealthy. They simply found and killed the animals for the marketplace. Tanneries, distributors, and retailers made the bulk of the profit. The big loser was the alligator. Alligators large and small were removed from the American landscape literally by the millions, just like the bison. The impact on the species' presence as a symbol of nature in the South was devastating.

In some regions justification for removing individual alligators, especially the larger ones, came from another quarter. Mammal trappers complained that alligators reduced the abundance of animals they sought: muskrats, otters, and beavers. A drop in the trade in mammal pelts was blamed on predation by the carnivorous reptiles. The trappers were probably right to some extent. Alligators will eat all of these mammals; even today one fairly sure way to rid a southern pond of beavers is to introduce a large alligator. But whether alligators reduced the numbers of semiaquatic furbearing mammals to any appreciable extent compared with the mammal trappers themselves is doubtful. Thus emerges another element of the early American land ethic: blaming a native species for an environmental problem that did not exist before human exploitation.

By the middle of the twentieth century the alligator's contribution to human civilization through the use of its skin for leather products and its victimization for other reasons had reduced it from the dominant creature of southern lowlands to a rarely seen curiosity. And the survivors were given no respite from injury or slaughter by anyone who knew how to use a gun or an ax. Some believe that the enactment and enforcement of the Endangered Species Act (1973) and other federal and state regulatory measures saved the American alligator from virtual extinction, an event that would have left a permanent blemish on the character of the people of North America.

But the emphasis on destroying the alligator should not be placed solely on killing individual animals. A more pervasive destructive force may prove more difficult to control and ultimately be more deleterious: the modification of the alligator's natural habitat through wetland degradation. The alligator is a keystone species in the aquatic habitats within its range, controlling population levels of prey and altering the habitat by making trails through terrestrial vegetation and dens beneath the banks. Thus the influence on alligators of people and their culture of development reverberates throughout the natural wetland ecosystems where alligators normally hold the franchise.

The draining of swamps and marshes, the damming of almost all the major southern rivers, and the clearing and removal of wetland vegetation have all contributed to reducing the alligator's natural habitat. The full impact is often not recognized because of the alligator's ability to adapt to artificial lakes, ponds, and canals, as well as its capacity to persist in areas heavily populated by people. Their obvious presence in such unnatural aquatic systems gives an illusion that alligators are coping with the human alteration of wetland habitat. And they probably are doing so more effectively than most wetland species they normally coexist with.

Although no conclusive data are available, a safe hypothesis is that under natural conditions fewer alligators inhabit areas after commercial and residential development than before, and that the overall effect is to reduce the potential habitat available for the American alligator. Despite the alligator's remarkable capacity to live in small numbers in aquatic systems even in urban areas, none can survive when wetlands are replaced with an agricultural field, a shopping mall, or an apartment complex.

Even more subtle influences on the natural history of the alligator can result from varying the spatial and temporal patterns of water fluctuations that are natural for a region. Such variations have been caused by redirecting water flows and controlling discharge timing and amounts. As Frank Mazzotti and Laura Brandt state, "Alligators are not doing well in the Everglades."[8] The degeneration of alligators in the Everglades is characterized by a suite of natural history traits—including growth rates, clutch sizes, and nesting frequencies—that are below what has been observed in other parts of the alligator's range.

Mazzotti and Brandt acknowledge two major causes for the deterioration of the Everglades aquatic systems. First, they cite "the drainage of wetlands south of Lake Okeechobee for agriculture and along the eastern fringe for residential development." Second, they note that the remaining marshes in the region are being altered by hydrological fluctuations that are incompatible with the optimal nesting and feeding requirements of alligators.[9]

The old American land ethic comes into play on an even broader scale—an entire geographic region. The purpose of development was not to intentionally disrupt the natural system, but to meet the immediate requirements and desires of an expanding human population, most notably in southern Florida, where the natural resources have been used and modified, often without people's realizing or caring that they were also being abused and mistreated. On the optimistic side, the American land ethic is changing in this arena. More and more people are beginning to understand and accept that to ensure a healthy society and economy, we must also maintain a healthy natural environment. Our standard-bearer for a new American land ethic remains Aldo Leopold, who wrote, "That land is a community is the

8. Frank J. Mazzotti and Laura A. Brandt, "Ecology of the American Alligator in a Seasonally Fluctuating Environment," in *Everglades: The Ecosystem and Its Restoration*, ed. S. M. Davis and J. C. Ogden (Delray Beach, Fla.: St. Lucie Press, 1994), p. 498.
9. Ibid.

basic concept of ecology, but that land is to be loved and respected is an extension of ethics."[10]

Let us assume that McIlhenny was wrong when he stated in 1935 that "it is extremely doubtful if [alligators] ever again will be an attractive feature of our waterways, as they were during the latter part of the last century." Let us proceed instead with the idea, and the plan, that alligators will once again become, as he viewed them at the turn of the twentieth century, "one of the most picturesque features of our lakes, rivers and bayous."[11] And let us hope they will remain so.

We have proven that a balanced and sustainable relationship between alligators and people is achievable in the climate of today's environmental attitudes. If we can maintain this model for the American land ethic of the twenty-first century, future generations of people and alligators should be granted the honor of sharing the American continent with each other.

10. Aldo Leopold, *A Sand County Almanac, with Essays on Conservation from Round River* (New York: Ballantine Books, 1966), p. xix. Leopold first espoused this idea, however, in his 1933 article in the *Journal of Forestry*; see Charles E. Little, *Hope for the Land* (New Brunswick, N.J.: Rutgers University Press, 1992), pp. 6–14.
11. McIlhenny, p. 25.

J. Whitfield Gibbons

Living
with Alligators

Blackwater

The dark waters of the Withlacoochee River seem fathomless, like a moonless night sky, but in the sunlight they sparkle like stars at night. Pure spring water looks blue, but as it mixes with groundwater stained by tannin from leaf litter and decaying vegetation, it is transformed into southern blackwater. In wetlands with abundant water plants, water tends to be clear unless polluted by fertilizers, which turn it into a green or brown soup. Pesticide residues from surrounding agricultural, industrial, and residential sources find their way into many streams and lakes. In concentrated doses, these toxic chemicals can kill aquatic life outright. Even small amounts can disrupt animals' reproduction by mimicking estrogen, an important female reproductive hormone. In Lake Apopka, poor hatching of alligator eggs and thus a population crash have been linked to pesticide pollution. In other wetlands exotic plants have burgeoned in an environment with few natural enemies, choking waterways and building up sludge as they decompose. When we tamper with fragile ecosystems, we disturb the life cycles of the inhabitants of the waterways.

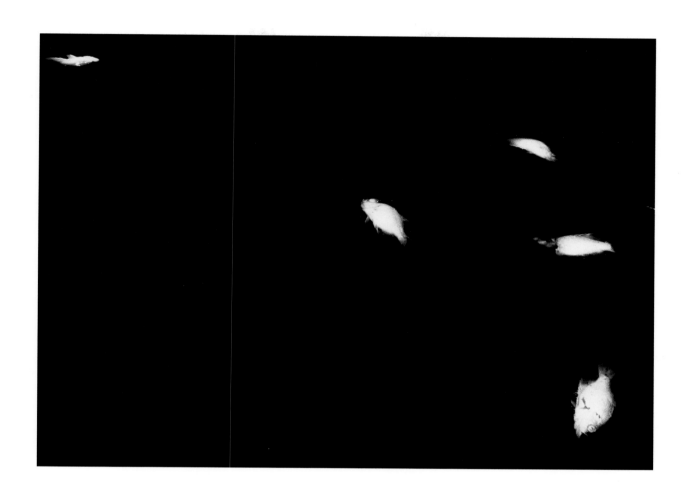

Eyeshine   *Martha A. Strawn*

Eyes above the waterline
mirror brilliant colors:
males, yellow-red
females, bluish yellow?

Plants part where alligators
course, seeking echoes
of their young who
sound out across the wetlands

Tealike blackwater conceals
a dinosaurian body floating
beneath the sparkling surface
of the tannic brew.

With aquatic grace, swift and smooth.
The hunter becomes the prey
as owls watch the biotic cycle,
ever changing, ever the same.

Wetlands and Deepwaters

The southern aquatic habitats are where alligators dwell. The long-range future of the alligator and its habitat is a continuing struggle for survival in the context of the encroachment of agricultural and urban use. *Sustainable use* conservation programs can help place *nature* on the list of economic assets and take it off the list of economic liabilities for existing and future development within the southeastern United States. The issue is not whether to support the concept but how the concept is to be instituted and governed. Who is included and who is left out by virtue of administration? What pressures do administrators contend with, and how are resolutions made?

The ideal is reachable on higher and lower levels of discourse and behavior. *Nature and culture,* not *nature versus culture*. The earth is the habitat of us all. The little decisions we make every day and the things we do and buy combine to create the larger ethic we aspire to support—an American land ethic that applies not only to the land, but also to the biotic systems of which it is a part.

Meditation   *Diane Ackerman*

Alligators are creatures of the water's edge
who have dual citizenship in the wet and dry
worlds. Though not technically amphibians,
They live in a similar twilight of water
and sky, and they are masters of the narrow
realm where the two worlds collide.[62]

![Wetlands logo] **Wetlands**

▌▐▌ Coda
Habitats and their living natural resources are under increasing pressure from market economies. Species, the basic units, are increasingly threatened with extinction as such economies grow in strength and expand into fragile ecosystems. But these economies need not operate at the expense of biotic survival: there are other options based on sustainable use in which local or indigenous communities take responsibility for the natural resources their livelihoods and lifeways have come to depend on. Those establishing resource management programs to protect and conserve biodiversity from species level to ecosystem need an understanding of land and life beyond biological sciences. Knowledge of local cultures, environmental economies, and governmental structures and dynamics—and an appreciation for the role of beauty in life—is also needed to establish an effective biotic support system.

The prehistoric presence of the alligator in the American landscape is an alluring living symbol for our continuing existence through time. Its dinosaurian form reminds us of our connections to the past; its fascinating demeanor and sheer physical power capture our attention now; and its amazing adaptability forecasts its continuance into the future. Mysterious crocodilian that it is, the alligator is part of our biotic cycle, just as we are part of the alligator's.

Only humans and other alligators are predators of the adult alligator. Intelligent people have the ability to consider the wisdom of perpetuating the full ecosystem and to make balanced use of sustainable resources for their own health and continuance in the cycle. The well-being of each of our lifelines lies in the exercise of our collective wisdom as we reflect on alligators and an American land ethic. It is as the American photographer and conservationist Ansel Adams once wrote:

Who can define the moods of the wild places, the meaning of nature in domains beyond those of material use? Here are worlds of experience beyond the world of the aggressive man, beyond history and beyond science. The moods and qualities of nature and the revelations of great art are equally difficult to define; we can grasp them only in the depths of our perceptive spirit.[63]

Notes

"Wetlands" is a single term that has been used to refer to landscape units describing a demarcation between dry and wet environments. Because reasons or needs for defining wetlands vary, many definitions have arisen. A recent redefinition used by state agencies and researchers for the purposes of inventory, evaluation, and mnangement divides aquatic environments into wetlands and deepwater habitats. Wetlands are lands transitional between terrestrial and aquatic systems where the water table in usually at or near the surface or the land is covered by shallow water. Deepwater habitats are permanently flooded lands lying below the deepwater boundary of wetlands. References in the photographs and text are self-evident. See Lewis M. Cowardin, Virginia Carter, Francis C. Golet, and Edward T. LaRoe, *Classification of Wetlands and Deepwater Habitats of the United States*, prepared for Office of Biological Services, Fish and Wildlife Service, U.S. Department of the Interior (Washington, D.C.: U.S. Government Printing Office, 1979).

1. The prevalent nomenclature for sibling groups of hatchling alligators is "pod," as used in David C. Deitz, "Behavioral Ecology of Young American Alligators" (Ph.D. diss., University of Florida, 1979), p. v. Another term used historically by William Bartram in his *Travels* is "brood": "The monster came up with the usual roar and menaces, and passed close by the side of my boat, when I could distinctly see a young brood of alligators to the number of one hundred or more, following after her in a long train, they kept close together in a column without straggling off to the one side or the other, the young appeared to be of an equal size, about fifteen inches in length, almost black, with pale yellow transverse waved clouds or blotches, much like rattle snakes in colour." *The Travels of William Bartram,* ed. with commentary and annotated index by Francis Harper (New Haven: Yale University Press, 1958), pp. 80–81.

2. There are two scientific theories about perched lakebeds in this area: that a meteor made a depression, and that the sea was originally farther inland and, retreating, left cradles of water higher than the surrounding land. This second theory is supported by the discovery of sea fossils in these inland areas.

3. "General Information," *Alligator River National Wildlife Refuge: Hunting Regulations and Permit, 1993–94*, RF-43580-6-July (Washington, D.C.: Department of the Interior, U.S. Fish and Wildlife Service, 1993).

4. *Alligator Management Plan: Executive Summary* (Gainesville: Florida Game and Fresh Water Fish Commission, 1984); and Ted Joanen, Larry MeNeese, Guthrie Perry, David Richard, and Dave Taylor, *Louisiana's Alligator Management Program,* Proceedings of the Annual Conference of Southeast Fish and Wildlife Agencies (n.p.: Louisiana Department of Wildlife and Fisheries, 1984).

5. Amos Cooper and Monique Slaughter, comps., *Annual Report: Population and Harvests of Alligators (*Alligator mississipiensis*)* *in Texas* (Austin: Texas Parks and Wildlife Department, 1993; updated to January 1995); Ted Joanen, Larry McNease, Guthrie Perry, and David Richard, *Louisiana's Alligator Management Program* (Grand Chenier: Louisiana Department of Wildlife and Fisheries, 1984); and Dave Taylor, Abstract for 1984 Proceedings of the Annual Conference of Southeast Fish and Wildlife Agencies (n.p.: Louisiana Department of Wildlife and Fisheries), pp. 201–11.

6. A. S. McQueen and Hamp Mizell, *History of Okefenokee Swamp* (Tallahassee, Fla.: Rose Printing Company, 1926; reprinted Folkston, Ga.: Charlton County Historical Society, 1992); and *My Life in the Okefenokee: Okefenokee Joe* (Decatur, Ala.: Black Water Music Company and Duck Tape Music, 1993).

7. Joseph T. Shipley, *Dictionary of Word Origins* (New York: Dorset Press, 1945), p. 101.

8. For further commentary see J. E. Cirlot, *A Dictionary of Symbols,* 2d ed., trans. Jack Sage (New York: Philosophical Library, 1971), pp. 67, 158–59.

9. *Omni*, November 1993; *New Yorker*, 31 May 1993.

10. *Paynes Prairie State Preserve* (Tallahassee: Florida Department of Natural Resources Division of Recreation and Parks, n.d.), pamphlet.

11. Will McLean, "Tate's Hell," in *Florida Sand: Original Songs and Stories of Florida* (Floral City, Fla.: Will McLean Foundation, 1987; reprinted 1990). Reproduced here with the permission of the Will McLean Foundation, P.O. Box 696, Floral City, Fla., 36236.

12. "History of the Central and Southern Florida Project," lecture script, facsimile, sent 7 April 1995 from Dennis Duke, U.S. Army Corps of Engineers, Jacksonville District. All subsequent references to this history are self-evident in their context.

13. Ibid.; Doug Struck, "Florida's River of Grass Is Dying of Thirst: People Strain to Reverse the Damage," *Charlotte Observer,* 15 July 1990 (reprinted from *Baltimore Sun*).

14. Julie Lumpkin, *Tom Yawkey Wildlife Center* (Columbia: South Carolina Department of Natural Resources, 1994).

15. E. A. McIlhenny, *The Alligator's Life History* (Berkeley, Calif.: Ten Speed Press, 1987), pp. 16–17.

16. Larry Cameron told me about Will Alston's description in Davidson, North Carolina, in August 1994.

17. McIlhenny, *Alligator's Life History,* p. 17.

18. J. Hugh McDowell et al., "The Alligator's Rhodopsin: Sequence and Biochemical Properties," *Experimental Eye Research,* 1996, forthcoming.

19. A few cookbooks devoted to alligator recipes are available. *The Alligator Cookbook* was compiled and funded by the Division of Marketing, Florida Department of Agriculture and Consumer Services, in cooperation with Ashley Associates and the Louisiana Fur and Alligator Advisory Council, in the mid-1980s. The following books are described in Vaughn L. Glasgow, *A Social History of the American Alligator* (New York: St. Martin's Press, 1991): *A Herpetological Cookbook: How to Cook Amphibians and Reptiles,* by Ernie Liner, was privately published in 1978 and contains twenty-five recipes for cooking alligator. In 1980 two alligator specialty cookbooks were published: *Gator* was edited and privately published by Tom and Barbara Malik, and the *Alligator Festival Cookbook* was published by the West St. Charles Rotary Club. In 1982 the International Alligator Festival in Franklin, Louisiana, published *Gator Gourmet.* Glasgow also cites *The Alligator Cookbook,* published by the National Alligator Association in Orlando, Florida, but gives no date. In his chapter titled "Survival Stew to Scallopini: The Edible Alligator," Glasgow gives insightful information about cuts and preparation of alligator meat, interesting culinary history, and tasty bits of relevant trivia.

20. Don Ashley, "Market Outlook and Industry Overview," *Gatortales: Florida Alligator Trappers Association Newsletter,* August 1993, pp. 3–4 (currently published by the American Alligator Cycle of Protection, P.O. Box 1637, Dade City, Florida 33526-1637).

21. Harry A. Kersey Jr., *Pelts, Plumes, and Hides: White Traders among the Seminole Indians, 1870–1930* (Gainesville: University Presses of Florida, 1975), pp. 58–72.

22. The Seminoles made a starch that they stored for times of famine. This starch, made from the wild zamia root, is known by several names, including kunti, coontie, and compte. Ibid., pp. 30, 52, and 116.

23. Ibid., p. 117.

24. Ibid., p. 76.

25. Ibid., p. 63.

26. Duke, "History of the Central and Southern Florida Project." Subsequent references to this history are self-evident in their context.

27. From *1992–93 Hunting and Fishing Maps for North Carolina Game Lands* (Raleigh: North Carolina Wildlife Resources Commission, 1992), back cover.

28. Commentary on Laura Grosch's asking Gill Holland to write a poem about water, 12 December 1994, Davidson, North Carolina.

29. *A Visitor's Guide to Matagorda Island State Park: An Island Park* (Austin: Texas Parks and Wildlife Department, 1991).

30. *The Handbook of Texas,* vol. 1 (Houston: Texas State Historical Association, 1986), p. 938; and W. W. Newcomb, *The Indians of Texas: From Prehistoric to Modern Times* (Austin: University of Texas Press, 1961), pp. 341–42.

31. T. Lindsay Baker, *Lighthouses of Texas* (College Station: Texas A&M University Press, 1991), p. 28; and Wayne H. McAlister and Martha K. McAlister, *Matagorda Island: A Naturalist's Guide* (Austin: University of Texas Press, 1993), p. 70.

32. See *1993 International Coastal Cleanup U.S. National Results* (Washington, D.C.: Center for Marine Conservation, 1993). Established in 1972, the Center for Marine Conservation is a nonprofit organization dedicated to the health of the marine environment. Its regional offices are in California, Florida, and Virginia. Thirty-nine countries participated in the International Coastal Cleanup. Further information about the organization or about the coastal cleanup results is available from the Center for Marine Conservation, 1725 DeSales Street NW, Suite 500, Washington, D.C.; telephone: 202-429-5609, fax: 202-872-0619.

33. Consultation with Allan R. Woodward, biologist, Alligator Specialist Group, Florida Game and Fresh Water Fish Commission, Gainesville, Florida, May 1995.

34. *The Natural Role of Fire*, Forestry Report R8-FR-15 (Tallahassee: Florida Department of Agriculture and Consumer Services, Division of Forestry, 1989).

35. Kersey, *Pelts, Plumes, and Hides,* p. 129.

36. Michael J. Caduto and Joseph Bruchac, *Keepers of the Animals: Native American Stories and Wildlife Activities for Children* (Golden, Colo.: Fulcrum, 1991), pp. xx, 193–94; and George E. Lankford, comp. and ed., *Native American Legends: Southeastern Legends Tales from the Natchez, Caddo, Biloxi, Chickasaw, and Other Nations* (Little Rock, Ark.: August House, 1987), p. 122.

37. Kevin Bezner, "Marsh," in *About Water* (Lemon Cove, Calif.: Dry Crik Press, 1993), p. 18.

38. *St. Marks National Wildlife Refuge: Florida* RF-41640-1-October (Washington, D.C.: Department of the Interior, U.S. Fish and Wildlife Service, 1987).

39. "Wakulla River," in *Florida Rivers Assessment* (Tallahassee: Florida Department of Environmental Protection, 1990); and *Myakka River State Park* (Tallahassee: Florida Department of Natural Resources, Division of Recreation and Parks, n.d.).

40. The state of Florida's document titled *The Florida Rivers Assessment* is an excellent and concise resource For further information of any of Florida's rivers. Each river is fully documented and mapped, and the keys identify the quality and character of the river in stages along its length. Write to Steven W. Martin, Mail Station 599, Department of Environmental Protection, 3900 Commonwealth Blvd., Tallahassee, Florida, 32399-3000.

41. Robert L. Dressler, David W. Hall, Kent D. Perkins, and Norris H. Williams, *Identification Manual for Wetland Plant Species of Florida* (Gainesville: Institute of Food and Agricultural Sciences, Florida Agricultural Experiment Station, Florida Cooperative Extension Service, and University of Florida, October 1987), p. 45; and Liberty H. Bailey, *Hortus Third: A Concise Dictionary of Plants Cultivated in the United States and Canada* (New York: Macmillan, 1976).

42. Jeffrey W. Lang and Harry V. Andrews, "Temperature-Dependent Sex Determination in Crocodilians," *Journal of Experimental Zoology* 270 (1994): 28–44.

43. Tim Williams, "Why Alligators?" *Gatortales: Florida Alligator Trappers Association Newsletter* 1, no. 2 (January 1994): 5.

44. *Rockefeller Refuge: Haven for Wildlife,* rev. ed., Wildlife Education Bulletin 105 (Baton Rouge: Department of Wildlife and Fisheries of Louisiana, 1982).

45. John Thorbjarnarson, *Crocodiles: An Action Plan for Their Conservation,* ed. Harry Messel, F. Wayne King, and James Perran Ross (Gland, Switzerland: IUCN/SSC Crocodile Specialist Group, International Union for Conservation of Nature and Natural Resources, 1992), pp. 5–6.

46. Value-added conservation means that the economic value of the animal is used to encourage the conservation of wetlands as well as to support animal management and research programs.

47. Looking at comparative bird books, Violet Crews was unsure what kind of bird a pond scoggin would be. "Pond scoggin" is the name her mother always used. In "A Sight of Alligators," in *Okefinokee Album,* Robert Allen Chesser (1859–1929), tells about scoggins: "I reckon there was five or six hundred birds around the edge of that lake-scoggins [herons], blue and white ones, and all kinds." Francis Harper and Delma E. Presley, *Okefinokee Album* (Athens: University of Georgia Press, Brown Thrasher Books, 1981), p. 94.

48. Hunters note that if an alligator is injured and rolls to the left it is not dead; if the alligator rolls to the left, then back to the right, or just rolls to the right, it's dead.

49. Jim Billie, "Big Alligator," *Native Son* (Fort Lauderdale, Fla.: Cumulus Nimbus Productions, 1986), courtesy of Bird Clan Publishing, American Society of Composers, Authors, and Publishers; and for understanding the stanzas in Seminole, refer to the first three lines of the song, which translate the refrain that runs throughout the song. *Hulpah-te cho-bee* means "big alligator."

50. "In North Carolina, the teeth of an alligator's right jaw (never the left)" were eaten (which must have been difficult unless they were powdered) by sterile or impotent male colonists, "to provoke Venery." Glasgow, *Social History of the American Alligator,* p. 4.

51. *American Alligator Cycle of Protection* (Dade City: Alligator Trappers Association of Florida, 1993), brochure.

52. Gill Holland, *The Tao Comes to Davidson* (Charlotte, N.C.: Briarpatch Press, 1994), pp. 94–95, reprinted with permission.

53. By "ecological stewardship" I mean stewardship that affects people, animals, and the land on natural and cultural levels.

54. James P. Pate, *The Fort Tombecbe Historical Research and Documentation Project,* with the assistance of William B. Stuart and Joe B. Wilkins Jr. (Livingston: Alabama Historical Commission and Livingston University, 1980), pp. 1, 43, 124–26, 153–56, 180–83, 199–200.

55. "Gator's Swoon Stalls Traffic for 90 Minutes," *Harrisonburg (Va.) Daily News-Record,* 17 June 1994, p. 8.

56. Dot Rees Gibson, "Okefenokee Pioneers: Lydia Smith Stone Crews, 'Queen of Cowhouse Island,'" in *The Okefenokee Swamp,* Historic Southern Classic Series no. 1 (Waycross, Ga.: Dot Gibson Publications, 1974), pp. 16–17.

57. "Wakulla River," in *Florida Rivers Assessment,* pp. 401–6.

58. A Florida Cracker is a native Floridian. Crackers are said to have "sand in their shoes," meaning that if they leave Florida they will yearn to return to the wetlands and sand hills covered with live oaks, palm trees, and citrus groves, the "land of flowers." See Lawrence E. Will, *A Cracker History of Okeechobee: Custard Apple, Moonvine, Catfish and Moonshine* (St. Petersburg, Fla.: Great Outdoors, 1964; reprinted Belle Glade, Fla.: Glades Historical Society, 1977), pp. 1–16.

59. Thomas H. Dyer, "Memorandum regarding `Initiative Summary,'" Two Rivers Ranch, Thonotosassa, Fla., sent to the Ecosystem Management Department/Role of the Private Landowners Committee at the request of the Ecosystem Management Department of the Florida Department of Environmental Protection (DEP) and the EMIS Committee, 15 March 1995, pp. 1–16; and "Final Report: Role of the Private Landowners Committee, Florida, Beginning Ecosystem Management," Private Landowners Committee, cochaired by Thomas H. Dyer and James R. Brindell, Thonotosassa and West Palm Beach, Fla., 20 October 1994, pp. 1–19, including attached tables and appendixes.

60. Robert M. Thomas, *A Message from Two Rivers,* as told to Richard D. R. Hoffman (Thonotosassa, Fla.: Two Rivers Ranch, [ca. 1990]), pp. 3–14.

61. Elizabeth Bishop, *The Complete Poems* (New York: Farrar, Straus and Giroux, 1969), pp. 35–36, reprinted with permission.

62. Holly Hughs, compiler, *Meditation on the Earth: A Celebration of Nature in Quotations, Poems, and Essays* (Philadelphia: Running Press, 1994), p. 199.

63. Ansel Adams, untitled essay insert, dedicated to Nancy and Beaumont Newhall, *Portfolio Three: Yosemite Valley* (San Francisco: Sierra Club, 1960).

Plates

Suggested Readings, Recordings, and Viewings

Readings

About Water. Kevin Bezner. Lemon Cove,Calif.: Dry Crik Press, 1993.

The Aesthetic Experience: An Anthropologist Looks at the Visual Arts. Jacques Maquet. New Haven: Yale University Press, 1986.

The Alligator: Monarch of the Marsh. Connie Toops. Homestead, Fla.: Florida National Parks and Monuments Association, 1988.

The Alligator's Life History. E. A. McIlhenny. Berkeley, Calif.: Ten Speed Press, 1987.

Alligators and Crocodiles. Malcolm Penny. New York: Crescent Books, 1991.

Another Way of Telling. John Berger and Jean Mohr. New York: First Vintage International, 1982; reprinted 1995.

Art as Culture. Evelyn Payne Hatcher. Lanham, Md.: University Press of America, 1985.

The Art of Scientific Investigation. W. I. B. Beveridge. New York: Vintage Books, 1960.

Artificial Nature. Jeffrey Deitch. Athens: Deste Foundation for Contemporary Art, 1990.

Between the Landscape and Its Other. Paul Vanderbilt. Baltimore: Johns Hopkins University Press, 1993.

Classification of Wetlands and Deepwater Habitats of the United States. Lewis M. Cowardin, Virginia Carter, Francis C. Golet, and Edward T. LaRoe, for Office of Biological Services, Fish and Wildlife Service, U.S. Department of the Interior. Washington, D.C.: U.S. Government Printing Office, 1979.

A Cracker History of Okeechobee: Custard Apple, Moonvine, Catfish, and Moonshine. Lawrence E. Will. Belle Glade, Fla.: Glades Historical Society, 1964; reprinted St. Petersburg, Fla.: Great Outdoors, 1977.

The End of Nature. Bill McKibben. New York: Doubleday, Anchor Books, 1990.

Ethical Land Use: Principles of Policy and Planning. Timothy Beatley. Baltimore: Johns Hopkins University Press, 1994.

The Everglades: River of Grass. Marjory Stoneman Douglas. St. Simons Island, Ga.: Mockingbird Books, 1947; reprinted 1991.

Eyelids of Morning: The Mingled Destinies of Crocodiles and Men. Alistair Graham and Peter Beard. Greenwich, Conn.: New York Graphic Society, 1973.

Feminism and Geography: The Limits of Geographical Knowledge. Gillian Rose. Minneapolis: University of Minnesota Press,1993.

Florida: Land of Fortune. Stephen J. Flynn. Washington, D.C.: Luce, 1962.

Gator Gourmet. Margie Laws Luke, ed. Franklin, La.: International Alligator Festival, 1982.

Green Delusions: An Environmentalist Critique of Radical Environmentalism. Martin W. Lewis. Durham, N.C.: Duke University Press, 1992.

Homo Aestheticus: Where Art Comes from and Why. Ellen Dissanayake. New York: Free Press, 1992.

Hope for the Land. Charles E. Little. New Brunswick, N.J.: Rutgers University Press, 1992.

Keepers of the Animals: Native American Stories and Wildlife Activities for Children. Michael J. Caduto and Joseph Bruchac. Golden, Colo.; Fulcrum, 1991.

Keeping All the Pieces: Perspectives on Natural History and the Environment. Whit Gibbons. Washington, D.C.: Smithsonian Institution Press, 1993.

Landscape in America. George F. Thompson, ed. Austin: University of Texas Press, 1995.

Native American Legends: Southeastern Legends-Tales from the Natchez, Caddo, Biloxi, Chickasaw, and Other Nations. Compiled and edited by George E. Lankford. Little Rock, Ark.: August House, 1987.

Okefinokee Album. Francis Harper and Delma E. Presley. Athens: University of Georgia Press, BrownThrasher Books, 1981.

Pelts, Plumes, and Hides: White Traders among the Seminole Indians, 1870–1930. Harry A. Kersey Jr. Gainesville: University Presses of Florida, Florida Atlantic University Book, 1975.

Poetics of Space: A Critical Photographic Anthology. Steve Yates, ed. Albuquerque: University of New Mexico Press, 1995.

The River Home: A Return to the Carolina Low Country. Franklin Burroughs. Boston: Houghton Mifflin, 1992. Originally published as *Horry and the Waccamaw* (New York: W. W. Norton, 1992).

A Sand County Almanac. Aldo Leopold. Oxford: Oxford University Press, 1949.

The Social Creation of Nature. Neil Evernden. Baltimore: Johns Hopkins University Press, 1992.

A Social History of the American Alligator. Vaughn L. Glasgow. New York: St. Martin's Press, 1991.

Suwanee River: Strange Green Land. Cecile Hulse Matschat. New York: Literary Guild of America, 1938.

The Tao Comes to Davidson. Gill Holland. Charlotte, N.C.: Briarpatch Press, 1994.

The Tao of Art. Ben Willis. London: Century, Rider Books, 1987.

Travels of William Bartram. Edited with commentary and annotated index by Francis Harper. New Haven: Yale University Press, 1958.

Wildlife Management: Crocodiles and Alligators. Grahame J. W. Webb, S. Charlie Manolis, and Peter J. Whitehead, eds. Chipping Norton, N.S.W.: Surrey Beatty and Sons, in association with Conservation Commission of the Northern Teritory, 1987.

Recordings

"Alligator." Charlie Daniels Band, *Homesick Blues*. Epic, 1988.

"Alligator." Various artists: Joe Louis Walker, *Blue Soul,* Hightone, 1989; Green Apple Quick Step, *Reloaded,* Medicine, 1995; Grateful Dead, *Anthem of the Sun,* Warner Brothers Records, 1971; Lester West, *Alligator,* IRS/CEMA, n.d.; Young Soldiers, *Alligator* (maxi single), Pump, 1993.

"Alligator and Kangaroo," Pheeroan ak Laff, *Sonogram,* Mu Records, 1990.

"The Alligator." Weird Al Yankovic and Wendy Carlos, *Peter and the Wolf/Carnival of the Animals: Prokofiev*. CBS Masterworks, 1990.

"Alligator Bait." Flowerpot Men, *The Peel Sessions (EP)*. Dutch East India, 1986.

"Alligator Blues." Helen Humes, *The Slide Guitars,* Legacy Records, 1993; Bay City Jazz Band, *The Bay City Jazz Band,* Good Time Jazz, 1956.

"Alligator Boogaloo." Lou Donaldson, *Blue Note 50th Anniversary Box Gift,* Blue Note Records, n.d.; *Jazz Super Hits of the '60's,* CEMA Special Products, 1992; Clarence "Gatemouth" Brown, *Alright Again!* Rounder Records, 1982.

"Alligator Crawl." Various artists: Fats Waller on albums under RCA Bluebird, 1987, Classics, n.d., Stash Records, 1991; Guy Van Duser under Rounder Records, n.d.; Louis Armstrong under Columbia and Laser Light, n.d., and Bella Musica, 1991; Canadian Brass under RCA Victor, 1992; and Les Brown and the Duke Blue Devils under Laser Light, n.d.

"Alligator Dance." Various artists, *Songs of Earth, Water, Fire, and Sky*. New World, n.d.

"Alligator Dancing King and Moore." Various artists, *Justice Records Sampler 2*, Justice Records, 1993; *Potato Radio*, Justice Records, 1992.

"Alligator Eating Dog." Clarence "Gatemouth" Brown, *No Looking Back*. Alligator Records, 1992.

"Alligator Head." Various artists, *Relix Records Sampler no. 3*. Relix, n.d.

"Alligator Heart." Soundtrack, *Hardware*. Varese Sarabande, n.d.

"Alligator Hop." Louis Armstrong and King Oliver, *Louis Armstrong and King Oliver*. Milestone Records, 1992.

"Alligator Man." Jimmy C. Newman, *Cajun Music*. MCA Special Products, n.d.; *Louisiana Saturday Night*. Charly, n.d.; LeRoi Brothers, *Open All Night*. Profile Records, n.d.; Alex Chilton, *Live in London*, Line (import, Germany), 1983.

"Alligator Meat." Joe Swift, *The Swingtime Records Story*. Capricorn, 1994.

"Alligator Shoes." Michael Dowdle, *From the Hip*. Airus, 1991.

"Alligator Shuffle." Lazy Lester, *Harp and Soul*. Alligator Records, n.d.

"Alligator Stomp." Pell Mell, *Bumper Crop*. SST, 1987; The Cramps, *Look Mom No Head*, Restless, 1991.

"Alligator Tail Drag." Wynton Marsalis, soundtrack for *Tune in Tomorrow. . . .* Columbia, 1990.

"Alligator Wine." Screamin' Jay Hawkins, *Live and Crazy*, Evidence, 1988; *Cowfingers and Mosquito Pie*, Legacy Rock Artifacts Series, 1991; *Voodoo Jive*, Rhino Records, 1990; *Real Life*, Charly, n.d.

"Alligator Wrestler." Sandy Bull, *Vehicles*. Timeless, n.d.

"Alligators." Willie "Loco" Alexander and . . . , *Willie "Loco" Alexander and His Persistent*. Accurate Distortion, 1993.

"Alligators All Around." Carole King, *A Natural Woman*, Legacy Records, 1994; *Really Rosie*, Columbia, 1975.

"Alligatory Crocodile." Ray Anderson, *What Because*, Gramavision Records, n.d.; *Brass Drum Bone, Wooferlo*, Soul Note, 1989.

"Alligatory Pecadillo." Ray Anderson Alligatory Band, *Don't Mow Your Lawn*. Enja, 1994.

"Amos Moses." Jerry Reed, *The Best of Jerry Reed*. BMG Music, 1992.

"The Battle of New Orleans." Johnny Horton, *Johnny Horton's Greatest Hits*. CBS, Inc., 1987.

"Big Alligator." Chief Jim Billie, *Seminole Man*, Tomorrow's Stars, 1992; *Native Son*, Seminole Records, 1986.

"Chanson Legäres (7)." Soloist: Michael Piquemal, baritone, *Jacques Chailley: Melodies/Piquemal, Steyer, Norska*. REM Recording.

"Crocodile." XTC, *Nonesuch*. Geffen Records, 1992.

"Crocodile Dadee." Dade, *In the Shade*, Big World, n.d.

"Crocodile Dundee." YZ ["Wise"], *YZ EP*. Tuff City Records, 1991.

"Crocodile Rock." Elton John, *Don't Shoot Me, I'm Only the Piano Player*, Polydor, 1972C; also other albums under Polydor, 1976A/ 1974C, Rhino, London 1994, MCA Records 1972D/1990, JCI Associated, Original Sound Entertainment 1993, and Digital Compact Classics 1974C; various artists, *Twenty Explosive Dynamic Super Smash Hit Explosions*, Pravda, n.d.; Debbie Gibson, *Live in Concert*, Pioneer Artists Video, 1989.

"Crocodile Song." The Seegers, *Animal Folk Songs for Children and Others*. Rounder Records, n.d.

"Crocodile Tear." Misha Mengelberg Trip, *Who's Bridge* Avant, 1994.

"Crocodile Tears." Mumps, *Fatal Charm 1975– 1980: Brief History*, Eggbert Records, 1994; and *D.I.Y.: Blank Generation-The New York Scene*, Rhino Records, 1993; Lee Roy Parnell, *Lee Roy Parnell*, Arista Records, 1989.

"Crocodile Totem." Adam Plack and Honny Soames, *Winds of Warning*. Australian Music International, 1994.

"Crocodile Walk." John Mayall. *London Blues (1964–1969)* Deram, 1992.

"Do Not Feed the Alligators." Dream Warriors, *And Now the Legacy Begins.* 4th and Broadway/Island, 1991.

"Don't Feed the Alligators." Dan Gibson, *Solitudes Sampler.*Solitudes, 1989.

"Frog Gigging." Okefenokee Joe, *My Life in the Okefenokee.*Cowhouse Island Record Company, 1993.

"The Hazards of the Trade." Okefenokee Joe, *My Life in the Okefenokee.* Cowhouse Island Record Company, 1993.

"I Refuse Alligator Man." Hue and Cry, *Seduced and Abandoned.* Virgin, 1987.

"I'm a Woman." Koko Taylor, *The Earthshaker.* Alligator Records, 1978.

"It's a Cold Night for Alligators." Various artists, *Where the Pyramid Meets the Eye.* Sire Records, 1990.

"Louisiana Story: Acadian Songs and Dances Alligator and Coon." Virgil Thomson, 1896–1989, *Berlitz Passport: The Music of the USA.* Sony Masterworks.

"Never Smile at a Crocodile." Fred Penner, *Poco.* Children's Group, 1993.

"Night Train (Smooth Alligator)." Lionel Richie, *Dancing on the Ceiling.* Motown Records, n.d.

"Sardines et crocodiles." Ensemble: Chifonnie, *Anthologie de la chanson franáaise traditionnelle.* EPM Recording Company, n.d.

"See You Later, Alligator." Various artists; Bill Haley and His Comets, with albums under MCA Records, 1968, 1985, and 1995; Drive Archive, 1994; Bescol, n.d.; Bobby Charles with albums under Chess, 1994 and 1995; Gene Vincent with *Be-Bop-a-Lula*, Royal Collection, n.d.; Zachary Richard, *Zack's Bon Ton*, Rounder Records, n.d.; Jimmy Page, *Jimmy's Back Pages . . . The Early Years*, Sony Music Special Products, 1992. Children's versions appear under Kid Rhino, 1992 and 1994.

"Snakes and Alligators." Bill Cosby, *When I Was a Kid.* MCA Records, 1971A.

"Solid Alligators Yeast." Various Artists, *Teriyaki Asthma, Vols. 1–5.* C/Z, n.d.

"Swampwise." Okefenokee Joe, *My Life in the Okefenokee.* Cowhouse Island Record Company, 1993.

"Swampy the Dog, Skeeter the Cat, and Me." Okefenokee Joe, *My Life in the Okefenokee.* Cowhouse Island Record Company, 1993.

"Tate's Hell." Will McLean, *Florida Sand, Vol. 1: My Soul Is a Hawk.* Wakulla Music, Will McLean Foundation, 1991.

"There's Something Wrong with You." Screamin' Jay Hawkins, *Cowfingers and Mosquito Pie.* Sony Music Entertainment, 1991.

"Way out Here." Chief Jim Billie, *Seminole Man,* Tomorrow's Stars, 1992; *Native Son,* Seminole Records, 1986.

"The Wintertime Truce." Okefenokee Joe, *My Life in the Okefenokee.* Cowhouse Island Record Company, 1993.

Viewings

Alligator. VHS. Alligator Associates, 1980.

Dinosaur! VHS. Phillips Mark Productions, 1985.

Here Be Dragons: National Geographic-Crocodiles. VHS. National Geographic Society, 1990.

Just Cause. VHS. Warner Brothers, 1995.

Louisiana Story. Sixteen-millimeter film and VHS. Original film 1948.

Acknowledgments

Over the past nine years I have met and worked with many generous people, supporters of this project who were essential to its development and completion. With all my being, I am grateful for the tremendous gifts of intelligence, scientific and artistic information, subsistence in the field, technical support, creative exchange, advice, and camaraderie. To all of them: I thank you so very much.

Individuals and agencies have helped with this project. The first and biggest supporter and a continuing resource is Dennis David, director of the Alligator Management Program for the State of Florida. It was Dennis who worked with University of Florida photography students in 1986, who helped me develop my knowledge about crocodilians worldwide, and who has been an ongoing facilitator and mentor, arranging contacts and advising on the development of this work up to the present. Dennis and Allen R. Woodward, biologist and alligator specialist working for the Florida Game and Fresh Water Fish Commission, put me in touch with most of my further resources in the southern United States. This work was made possible by all their contributions in research support, professional consultation, and advice.

Others who have played significant roles by gathering information, doing visual fieldwork, providing inspiration, and offering other forms of professional support for this project are Lindsay Hoard (biologist, Florida Game and Fresh Water Fish Commission at Okeechobee), Jimmy McDaniel (director of wildlife for the Seminole Reservation lands, Florida), Ruth Elsey (director of the Alligator Management Program, Rockefeller National Wildlife Refuge, Louisiana), Phil Wilkinson, (biologist, state of South Carolina), Dick Frickland (retired investigative reporter for the *Washington Post* and world-class kayaker), Louie Waller Jr. (naturalist, Florida), John Boudreaux (alligator hunter, Louisiana), LeRoy Overstreet (nuisance control alligator hunter, Alabama), Rita Fagan (coowner and associate operator of Fagan Alligator Products, Florida), Mike Fagan (coowner and operator of Fagan Alligator Products and president of the American Alligator Cycle of Protection), Kathleen Veatch (biologist, Matagorda Island State Park), Terry Turney (biologist, J. D. Murphree National Wildlife Refuge), Phil Stone (game warden, Holly Shelter Game Lands), and James Beaseley (biologist, Alligator River National Wildlife Refuge, North Carolina). Without their contributions great chunks of information and experience would be missing. Special thanks to LeRoy Overstreet and Mike Fagan for their continued and extended contributions to diverse aspects of this project.

Additional contributions of subsistence support during the fieldwork, technical and research support, and personal support were generously provided by Louie and Vera Waller, Barbara and Kenneth Brice, Robin Hood Leach, Peter Bunnell, Allen Compton, Joe Smoke, Evon Streetman, Sita and Asoka Srinivasan, Tatum and Leroy Young, Alice and E. T. Guidry, Thomas Guidry, Estelle and Linton Thibodeaux, June Overstreet, Violet Crews, Cheryl Heaton, June Kimmel, Marjorie Vernon, Joan Tweedy, Jeanne Dutterer, Bonnie Phillips, Laura Grosch, Douglas Dalton Jr., Mike Jarmon, and Marion Strawn.

For contributions of facilities, resources, materials, and creative works I am grateful to Margaret Longhill, director of the Will McLean Foundation; Gill Holland, poet; the Florida Game and Fresh Water Fish Commission; Mike Fagan of Fagan Alligator Products; Gatorland; the St. Augustine Alligator Farm; the Anahuac (Texas) Chamber of Commerce; Kevin Bezner, poet; James Billie, chief of the Seminole tribe and songwriter; Lynn Lawhead, director, American Alligator Cycle of Protection; and Marianne Bresson, and the Kitty Hawk Outdoors Center.

This project has also been supported with funding from the University of North Carolina, Charlotte, and the North Carolina Arts Council. And special gratitude is extended to William E. Parker, who provided continuing artistic dialogue, critical assessment, and encouragement.

As important as all the contributors are, second to none is George F. Thompson, president of the Center for American Places and publishing consultant for the Johns Hopkins University Press. In 1988 I had just finished the first part of this project in Florida. In consultation with Dennis David I planned to broaden its scope to include all of the southern states inhabited by alligators. Then I planned to seek a publisher. I had an appointment with George about other work, and he asked me what I did in my spare time. I said "alligators and land." In Baltimore, over crabcake sandwiches and beer, George and I shook hands and decided to tackle this work together. He has been remarkable. George has amazing patience, energy, enthusiasm, and intelligence. He applies those attributes with great skill to creative publishing. He is an author's editor, and it has been my extreme pleasure to work with him. He has been a mentor, a facilitator, and a friend. As this work draws to a close, I hold George Thompson in highest esteem, and I am very grateful for that crabcake lunch!

Index

Martha A. Strawn was born in Washington, D.C., in 1945 and grew up in Lake Wales, Florida. She studied art and marine biology at Florida State University, receiving a B.S. in art, and she completed an M.F.A. in art at Ohio University School of Fine Arts. She also attended Brooks Institute of Photography and the Florida State University Graduate School of Asian Art History in Japan. She has devoted her life to creative research, teaching, and photography. In 1973 she cofounded a nonprofit photographic arts organization in Charlotte, North Carolina, that became known as The Light Factory, in which she is still active. She has served as director and board chair of The Light Factory, as chair of the Society of Photographic Education, and as a member of the board of directors of the Friends of Photography. She is currently on the board of directors of the Center for American Places. Her work is interdisciplinary and collaborative. Previous work includes *Threshold: Mazes, Mysticism, and the Female Principle in India*, produced in visual and written forms over an eleven-year period in conjunction with Indian women who study and practice making threshold diagrams. The project involved Indian and American scholars in religion, anthropology, and art history. For this work she was awarded a National Endowment for the Arts fellowship in 1980, support from the R. J. Reynolds Foundation in 1982, a Fulbright fellowship in 1984, and support from the University of North Carolina and the North Carolina Arts Council. Her work has been exhibited widely and is part of numerous collections, including the Princeton Art Museum and the Indira Gandhi Centre for the Arts, New Delhi. Since 1986 she has received support from the North Carolina Arts Council, the University of North Carolina, and the state of Florida for her work on landscape and the conservation of alligators and wetlands. She now lives in Davidson, North Carolina, and is a professor of art at the University of North Carolina in Charlotte.

LeRoy Overstreet was born in 1925 in Sebring, Florida, and grew up near Kissimmee, Florida. He is a licensed general contractor whose specialties are building factories and doing commercial diving for salvage and construction. He learned most of what he knows about alligator hunting from Rossie Clemens when he was fourteen years old. In the late 1950s he married June Overstreet and moved to Texas, then to Mississippi in the 1960s and to Alabama in January 1972. He became a nuisance gator hunter for the state of Alabama in 1990, covering Pickens, Sumter, Greene, Tuscaloosa, Marengo, and Choctaw Counties. When he was injured in a construction accident he got bored sitting around with nothing to do, so he started writing. He still works as a nuisance control hunter and owns and operates Little River Construction Company in Epes, Alabama.

Jane Gibson was born in Waco, Texas, in 1954, where she also grew up. She received a B.A. in anthropology and environmental studies and an M.A. in environmental studies from Baylor University and completed a Ph.D. in anthropology at the University of Florida. Her specialties include race, ethnicity, and other sources of identity, ecological anthropology, natural resource management, economic anthropology, and visual anthropology, especially in the United States and Central America. Her articles have appeared in the *Kansas Journal of Law and Public Policy* and in *Human Organization*, among other peer-reviewed journals, and she has worked as a freelance photographer and journalist. Her visual work includes "Boots, Belts, and Baggage," an ethnographic video (1989) concerning relations of production in Florida's alligator industry. She is an assistant professor of anthropology at the University of Kansas, Lawrence.

J. Whitfield Gibbons was born in 1939 in Montgomery, Alabama, and grew up in Tuscaloosa. He received a B.S. and an M.S. in biology from the University of Alabama and completed a Ph.D. in zoology at Michigan State University. He has devoted his professional career to ecological research and teaching. His books include *Keeping All the Pieces: Perspectives on Natural History and the Environment* (Smithsonian Institution Press, 1993), *Guide to the Reptiles and Amphibians*, with Raymond D. Semlitsch (University of Georgia Press, 1991), *Poisonous Plants and Venomous Animals of Alabama*, with Robert R. Haynes and Joab L. Thomas (University of Alabama Press, 1990), *Life History and Ecology of the Slider Turtle* (Smithsonian Institution Press, 1990), and *Their Blood Runs Cold: Adventures of Reptile and Amphibians* (University of Alabama Press, 1983). He has also edited three books and has written chapters for publication in more than twenty others; his articles have appeared in more than a hundred peer-reviewed journals and occasionally in more popular publications such as *Natural History* magazine. He lives in Aiken, South Carolina, and is professor of ecology at the University of Georgia and senior research ecologist at the Savannah River Ecology Laboratory, University of Georgia. He is also a syndicated columnist for the *Tuscaloosa News*, a *New York Times* newspaper.

Library of Congress Cataloging-in-Publication Data

Strawn, Martha.

  Alligators, prehistoric presence in the American landscape /
Martha A. Strawn : with essays by LeRoy Overstreet, Jane Gibson,
J. Whitfield Gibbons.

    p. cm. — (Creating the North American landscape)

    Includes bibliographical references (p.) and index.

    ISBN 0-8018-5289-7

    1. American alligator—Southern States. 2. American alligator—
Southern States—Pictorial works. I. Title. II. Series.

QL666.C925S82 1997

597.98'0975—dc20   96-13762

Alligators, Prehistoric Presence in the American Landscape
by Martha A. Strawn

Designed by Glen Burris and set by the designer in Officina Sans,
Amasis, Blackoak, Madrone, Monotype Script, and Caravan orna-
ments. Separated and printed by C & C Offset Printing Company,
Ltd., Hong Kong.